Help your child to read and write: part 2

Sounds-Write Activity Book

Initial Code Units 8-11

by Tita Beaven and John Walker

SOUNDS-WRITE
First Rate Phonics

This book supports our online course <u>'Help your child to read and write – part 2'</u>, which can be found on the online learning platform Udemy. Join the parents and carers who have completed the course! Here's just one of several 5-star reviews:

> ★★★★★
> Great instructions, simple course - just what parents and their children need to learn to read and write

If you have an iPad, you might want to download our app 'Initial Code by Sounds-Write Ltd' from the Apple App Store (for use on iPads only). The app – which has been designed to introduce the sound-spelling correspondences in the Initial Code of the Sounds-Write programme - offers a variety of activities aimed at developing the skills of segmenting and blending, word reading and writing, and some sentence reading and writing. In addition to the full version, there is also a free version available which includes some sample lessons.

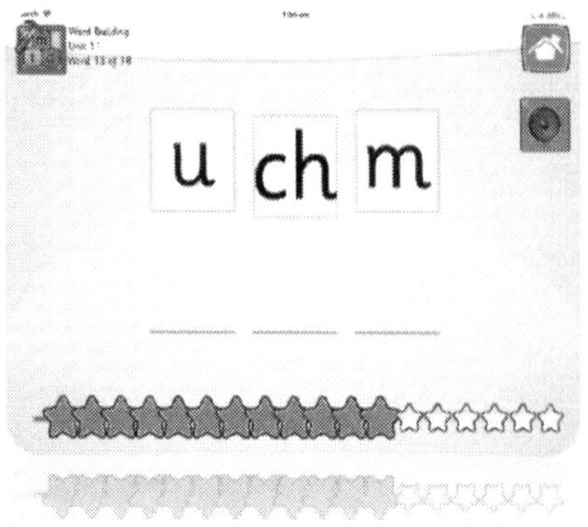

Introduction

We at Sounds-Write believe that learning to read and write is the single most important factor in early education because literacy provides a portal to all other kinds of learning.

This practice book has been written for parents and carers to enable them to help guide their children through the first steps in learning to read and write.

The book supports our online course 'Help your child to read and write – part 2', which can be found on the online learning platform Udemy. It is also designed for children who are learning to read using the Sounds-Write phonics programme at school, so that they can do additional practice both in school and at home. It follows on from the first book and video course in this series, 'Help your child to read and write – part 1', which cover the first 7 units of the Sounds-Write programme.

The book is intended primarily for parents and carers of children who are just beginning to learn to read and write and we strongly suggest that you take your child through the first course and supporting book before starting part 2. As you go through the book, if you find yourself unsure how to proceed, go back to the Udemy course to see how each lesson is taught and exactly what language to use.

In this book, you'll find a broad range of supplementary activities to accompany the programme. These include word building, word reading, sentence reading and dictation tasks, memory games, tracking and other activities. (Many of these will already be familiar to you if you have completed the online course.) Such activities aim at promoting the kind of practice essential to young children if they are going to become properly literate.

Each activity begins with simple instructions on how you and your child can work together to complete the task at hand. The activities have been mixed or 'interleaved', partly to keep up interest and partly because this helps to get the information being learned into long-term memory.

The activities for each unit are also broadly arranged from simple to more complex. It's not essential to do all of them with your child: if he or she is achieving around 75% to 80% accuracy on the current unit, you might want to move on to the next one.

Some of the activities involve you pointing to the letters when your child is reading. You can do this with a pencil but we prefer to use a chopstick, as it doesn't mark the book!

You might also be interested in our book *Phonic stories to read at home 2 (a phonics reader for Sounds-Write Initial Code Units 8 to 11)* which is available on Amazon in Kindle format.

The reader contains ten **decodable** stories for young children who are learning to read following the Sounds-Write phonics programme (Initial Code Units 8-11). Carefully following the Sounds-Write sequence, these engaging stories with their beautiful full-colour illustrations are written specifically for beginners. They enable children to develop and practise their phonic knowledge and skills in a gradual and systematic way. The stories carefully follow the Sounds-Write sequence to give children confidence and success.

Contents

Unit 8

<u>All sounds-spellings</u>: a, i, m, s, t, n, o, p, b, c, g, h, d, e, f, v, k, l, r, u, x, y, j, w, z

<u>Word structure</u>: VCC and CVCC

<u>High frequency words</u>: a, is, the, I, for, of, are, all, come, into

8.1 Word building (VCC)

Your child is going to build four VCC (vowel, consonant, consonant) words: 'elf', 'ant', 'imp' and 'and'. For the first word, 'elf', run your chopstick or pencil under the lines in the 'Build the word' box, saying the word very slowly. Don't segment it or separate the sounds. Make sure you are saying the sounds, not the letter names! Emphasise the missing sound by stretching it out (eeeeelf). Now ask your child to choose the correct spelling of the missing sound from the Sounds/Spellings box and write it on the line, saying the sound as they write it. Then ask them to write the word under the 'Write the word' column, saying the sounds as they do, and read the word. After that, do the same with the other words. With the word 'and' you can't really stretch the missing sound, /d/, so say it a bit louder ('anD').

Sounds/Spellings

n e d i

Build the word	Write the word
__ l f	__ __ __
a __ t	__ __ __
__ m p	__ __ __
a n __	__ __ __

8.2 Word building (CVCC)

Your child is going to build two CVCC (consonant, vowel, consonant, consonant) words: 'lift' and 'went'. For the first word, 'lift', run your chopstick under the lines saying the word very slowly. Don't segment it or separate the sounds. It's your child's job to identify the missing sound. Make sure you are saying the sounds, not the letter names! Emphasise the missing sound by stretching it out (liffffffft). As your child identifies the sound by saying it, ask them to choose the correct spelling of the missing sound from the Sounds/Spellings box and write it on the line, saying the sound as they write it. Then ask them to write the word, saying the sounds as they do, and read the word. After that, do the same with 'went'.

Sounds/Spellings:

f n

Build the word

l i ___ t

Write the word

___ ___ ___ ___

Build the word

w e ___ t

Write the word

___ ___ ___ ___

8.3 Word building (CVCC)

Your child is going to build four CVCC (consonant, vowel, consonant, consonant) words: 'help', 'vest', 'fond' and 'hump'. For the first word, 'help', run your chopstick under the lines under the 'Build the word' heading saying the word very slowly. Don't segment it or separate the sounds. It's your child's job to segment or separate the sounds in the word. Make sure you are saying the sounds, not the letter names! Now, as your child identifies each sound by saying it, ask them what the spelling is for that sound from the Sounds/Spellings box. Then ask them to write the spelling, saying the sound as they do. Do this with each sound-spelling correspondence, one at a time, until you get to the end of the word. Finally, ask your child to read the word. Then do the same with the other words.

Build the word

Sounds/Spellings
l e p h

___ ___ ___ ___

Build the word

Sounds/Spellings
e t v s

___ ___ ___ ___

Build the word

Sounds/Spellings
n d f o

___ ___ ___ ___

Build the word

Sounds/Spellings
u m p h

___ ___ ___ ___

8.4 Word building (CVCC)

Your child is going to build four CVCC (consonant, vowel, consonant, consonant) words: 'milk', 'rest', 'send' and 'mist'. For the first word, 'milk', run your chopstick under the lines under the 'Build the word' heading, saying the word very slowly. Don't segment it or separate the sounds. It's your child's job to segment or separate the sounds in the word. Make sure you are saying the sounds, not the letter names! Now, as your child identifies each sound by saying it, ask them what the spelling is for that sound from the 'Sounds/Spellings' box. When they have linked sound to spelling, ask them to write the spelling, saying the sound as they do. Do this with each sound-spelling correspondence until you get to the end of the word. Finally, ask your child to read the word. Then do the same with the other words.

Build the word

Sounds/Spellings
l k m i

___ ___ ___ ___

Build the word

Sounds/Spellings
e t r s

___ ___ ___ ___

Build the word

Sounds/Spellings
n d s e

___ ___ ___ ___

Build the word

Sounds/Spellings
s t m i

___ ___ ___ ___

8.5 Word building (CVCC)

Your child is going to build four CVCC (consonant, vowel, consonant, consonant) words: 'kilt', 'west', 'nuts' and 'lips'. For the first word, 'must', run your chopstick under the lines under the 'Build the word' heading saying the word very slowly. Don't segment it or separate the sounds. Make sure you are saying the sounds, not the letter names! It's your child's job to segment or separate the sounds in the word. Now, as your child identifies each sound by saying it, ask them what the spelling is for that sound from the 'Sound/Spellings' box. When they have linked sound to spelling, ask them to write the spelling, saying the sound as they do. Do this with each sound-spelling correspondence until you get to the end of the word. Finally, ask your child to read the word. Then do the same with the other words.

Build the word

Sounds/Spellings

l k t i

___ ___ ___ ___

Build the word

Sounds/Spellings

e t w s

___ ___ ___ ___

Build the word

Sounds/Spellings

n t s u

___ ___ ___ ___

Build the word

Sounds/Spellings

p s i l

___ ___ ___ ___

8.6 Word reading (VCC)

Your child is going to read some VCC (vowel, consonant, consonant) words. Ask them to say the sounds and read the word, and then to match it with the correct picture.

elf

act

elk

imp

ant

alp

8.7 Word reading and writing (CVCC)

Your child is going to read some CVCC (consonant, vowel, consonant, consonant) words. Ask them to say the sounds and read each of the words below. When they have read the word successfully, ask them to write it, saying the sounds as they do. When they have written the word, ask them to read it back once more, to make sure the word they wrote was the one they wanted to write.

fist ___ ___ ___ ___

maps ___ ___ ___ ___

hats ___ ___ ___ ___

hunt ___ ___ ___ ___

nest ___ ___ ___ ___

sand ___ ___ ___ ___

belt ___ ___ ___ ___

camp ___ ___ ___ ___

pest ___ ___ ___ ___

mist ___ ___ ___ ___

yelp ___ ___ ___ ___

8.8 Sentence reading

Ask your child to say the sounds and read each word in the sentence, and then match it with the correct picture.

Dusk sets in as the sun dips in the west.

Jeff left a lump of sand on the sink.

Dad had a rant at Stan and Stan went off in a sulk.

8.9 Tracking

Ask your child to find the target word by tracking along each line from left to right with a chopstick or a pencil.

bend

d n o f v b e d p s t i b e n d m a d b

vest

a n e b v e g p s t i v e t f v e s t m a

film

a i f i t p s f i l m a s n e d b n f m a

8.10 Sentence reading

Ask your child to say the sounds and read each word in the sentence, and then answer yes or no by looking at the picture. Remind them that we start a sentence with a capital letter, and that we use a question mark at the end of a question.

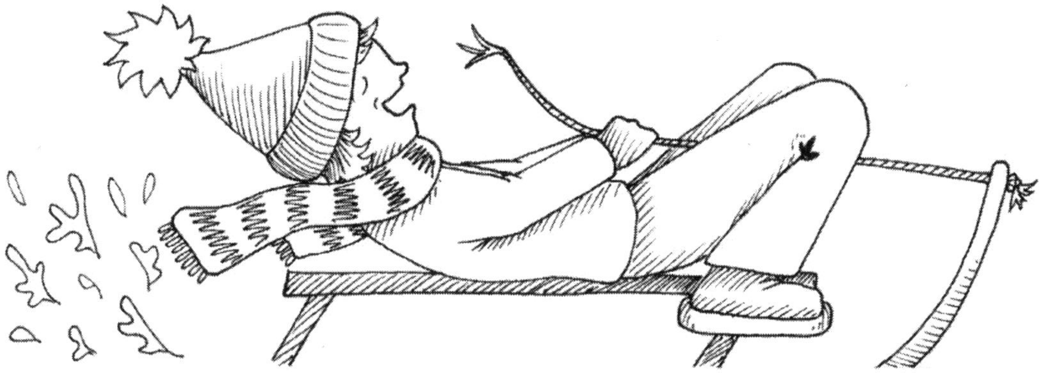

Is Ben's red hat in his left hand?

Is the runt a big piglet?

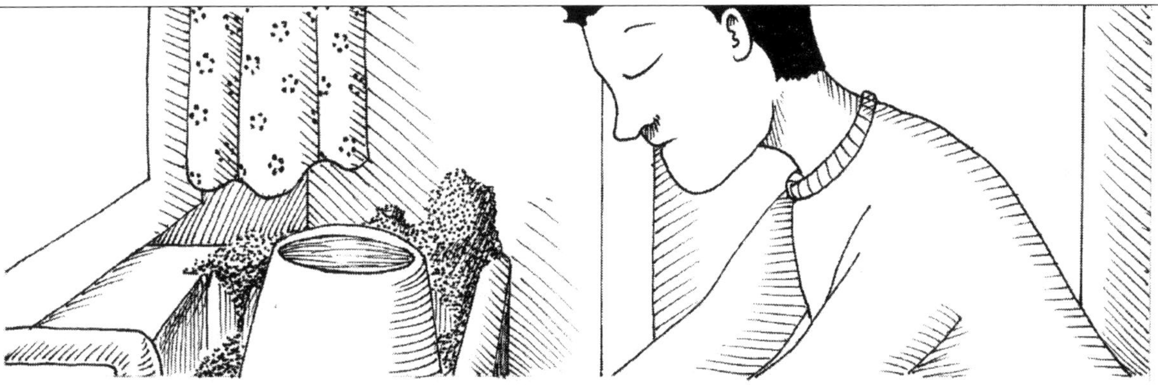

Did Dad get rid of the sand in the sink?

8.11 Cut and stick

Photocopy this page and cut up the words in each sentence. Working through one sentence at a time, ask your child to read each word and put them in order so they make sense. Then they can stick the words on a piece of paper. Once they've done that, get them to read the sentence again.

1

the	put	to	lamp.
in	Mum	on	went

2

Rolf	a	his	kept
in	tank.	pets	

3

Bess	to	sent	Mum.
help	Jeff		

8.12 Order and write (letters in words)

Ask your child to look at each picture, re-order the spellings and write the appropriate word, saying each sound as they write it. Then ask them to read the word.

e v t s	m a p c	i f g t

k e d s	t t e n	o p n d

8.13 Dictation

Tell your child you are going to read a sentence which they will then write on a piece of paper or a whiteboard. Firstly, read the whole sentence. Then read each word, one at a time, as your child writes it. Don't forget to remind them to say the sounds of each spelling in each word as they write. When they have written the whole sentence, ask them to read it. Don't do more than one sentence per day. You might have to write the word 'into' for your child, as this is a word they probably won't know how to spell yet.

1. Rex went limp as he let himself sink into the sand.

2. The big red dog sat next to Jan on the bank.

3. Did a gust of wind tip the box off the top of the bin?

4. The best bits of ham got left in the tin.

8.14 Tracing for handwriting practice

Ask your child to practise writing the spellings and saying the sounds as they write each one. They should not practise writing the sounds in isolation until they have completed the word building and other activities for the unit.

v v v v v v v v v

g g g g g g g g g

d d d d d d d d d

p p p p p p p p p

8.15 Speed read (CVCC)

How many CVCC (consonant, vowel, consonant, consonant) words can your child read in 20 seconds? Time them and keep a record of how many words they read correctly. You can repeat the activity several times to challenge them to read faster.

mint

band

desk

lamp

gift

gust

pant

mend

jest

tent

pump

tusk

rust

damp

Your record: **Day 1:** **Day 2:** **Day 3:** **Day 4:** **Day 5:**

8.16 Four in a row game

For the rules of the game, see page 165. Photocopy this page and use it as the board; also photocopy and cut up the counters on page 165.

hump	bulb	disk	dent	vest	silk	rusk	band
bump	cats	land	ramp	wimp	yank	bend	taps
gaps	lump	rusk	wind	mint	kept	jump	test
gulp	felt	camp	hand	silt	dusk	went	caps
limp	best	tank	punt	pals	fond	hips	left
lips	mist	nuts	rest	rips	silk	wept	wilt
west	dips	sand	dust	hunt	loft	belt	limp

8.17 Wordsearch

Ask your child to find the following words in the Wordsearch by tracking through each line from left to right. Every time they find a word, ask them to say the sounds and read the word.

band	belt	bend	bulb	cats	dusk
gaps	gulp	hips	hump	kept	land
loft	mint	nuts	tank	test	wept

b	e	f	h	u	m	p	u	j	b	a	n	d
a	b	u	l	b	l	a	n	t	g	a	s	p
k	e	p	d	e	l	t	c	a	t	s	e	s
l	a	n	d	u	l	b	e	n	d	t	a	n
a	g	a	p	s	h	i	s	p	s	a	t	s
b	h	u	m	i	n	t	e	n	k	e	p	t
b	a	n	b	e	n	t	e	s	t	o	p	d
m	g	u	l	p	d	u	s	k	e	q	t	o
n	i	n	t	u	p	l	t	a	n	k	i	s
w	e	n	s	l	i	f	t	n	u	t	o	m
h	i	p	s	a	l	a	f	t	e	t	s	a
g	a	p	s	i	p	l	e	n	t	l	a	n
k	t	a	n	c	o	l	n	u	t	s	o	m
f	w	e	p	t	f	o	l	t	l	o	f	t
n	e	s	t	o	b	e	l	t	p	a	l	f

Unit 9

New sounds-spellings: There are no new sound-spellings in this unit. The unit focuses on segmenting and blending CCVC words.

All sounds-spellings: a, i, m, s, t, n, o, p, b, c, g, h, d, e, f, v, k, l, r, u, x, y, j, w, z, ff, ll, ss, zz

Word structure: CCVC

High frequency words: a, is, the, I, for, of, are, all, come, some

9.1 Word building (CCVC)

Your child is going to build four CCVC (consonant, consonant, vowel, consonant) words: 'flag', 'slam', 'smell' and 'skip'. Do as you did before in Unit 8 and run your chopstick under the lines under the 'Build the word' heading saying the word very slowly. Don't segment it or separate the sounds. It's your child's job to segment or separate the sounds in the word. Make sure you are saying the sounds, not the letter names! Now ask your child to choose the correct spelling of the missing sound from the Sounds/Spellings box and write it on the line, saying the sound as they write it. Do this with each sound-spelling correspondence until you get to the end of the word. Finally, ask your child to read the word. Then do the same with the other words. With the word 'smell', you might have to remind your child that < ll > is two letters, but it is one sound.

Build the word

Sounds/Spellings

l g f a

Build the word

Sounds/Spellings

l a m s

Build the word

Sounds/Spellings

ll m s e

Build the word

Sounds/Spellings

s p i k

9.2 Word building (CCVC)

Your child is going to build four CCVC (consonant, consonant, vowel, consonant) words: 'slim', 'stuff', 'spell' and 'glad'. Do as you did before in Unit 8 and run your chopstick under the lines under the 'Build the word' heading saying the word very slowly. Don't segment it or separate the sounds. Make sure you are saying the sounds, not the letter names! Now ask your child to choose the correct spelling of the missing sound from the Sounds/Spellings box and write it on the line, saying the sound as they write it. Do this with each sound-spelling correspondence until you get to the end of the word. Finally, ask your child to read the word. Then do the same with the other words. With the word 'stuff' you might have to remind your child that < ff > is two letters, but it is one sound. The same applies to 'spell'.

Build the word

Sounds/Spellings
l s m i

___ ___ ___ ___

Build the word

Sounds/Spellings
u ff t s

___ ___ ___ ___

Build the word

Sounds/Spellings
ll p s e

___ ___ ___ ___

Build the word

Sounds/Spellings
g d a l

___ ___ ___ ___

9.3 Word building (CCVC)

Your child is going to build four CCVC (consonant, consonant, vowel, consonant) words: 'spot', 'blob', 'cliff' and 'twig'. Run your chopstick under the lines saying the word very slowly. Don't segment it or separate the sounds. Make sure you are saying the sounds, not the letter names! Now ask your child to choose the correct spelling of the missing sound from the 'Sounds/Spellings' box and write it on the line, saying the sound as they write it. Do this with each sound-spelling correspondence until you get to the end of the word. Finally, ask your child to read the word. With the word 'cliff' you might have to remind your child that < ff > is two letters, but it is one sound.

Build the word

Sounds/Spellings

p t s o

___ ___ ___ ___

Build the word

Sounds/Spellings

l o b b

___ ___ ___ ___

Build the word

Sounds/Spellings

i ff c l

___ ___ ___ ___

Build the word

Sounds/Spellings

w g i t

___ ___ ___ ___

9.4 Word reading (CCVC)

Your child is going to read some CCVC (consonant, consonant, vowel, consonant) words. Ask them to say the sounds and read the word, and then to match it with the correct picture.

slug

flag

twig

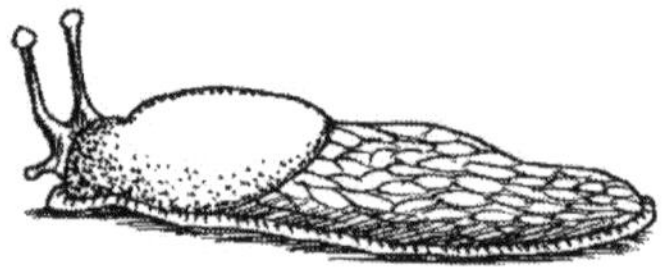

plum

skiff

pram

9.5 Word reading and writing (CCVC)

Your child is going to read some CCVC (consonant, consonant, vowel, consonant) words. Ask them to say the sounds and read each of the words below. When they have read the word successfully, ask them to write it, saying the sounds as they do. When they have written the word, ask them to read it back once more, to make sure the word they wrote was the one they wanted to write.

clap ___ ___ ___ ___

trap ___ ___ ___ ___

plug ___ ___ ___ ___

spin ___ ___ ___ ___

stag ___ ___ ___ ___

cliff ___ ___ ___ ___

fluff

bless

spill

sniff

press

9.6 Sentence reading

Ask your child to read each word in each of the sentences. If they can read the word without sounding out each sound, that's fine. Then ask them to read the sentence again, a bit more quickly this time. Finally, ask them to re-read the sentence once more, this time even more quickly.

1. Tom's twin, Stan, has a twig in his hand.

2. Glen must run to get some stuff from the camp.

3. Jill kept a frog, a slug and a crab in a tin drum.

9.7 Sentence reading

Ask your child to read each word in each of the sentences. If they can read the word without sounding out each sound, that's fine. Then ask them to read the sentence again, a bit more quickly this time. Finally, ask them to re-read the sentence once more, this time even more quickly.

1. Stan sent Jeff to get the maps from Mum.

2. Tom's twin Fred was ill. His mum felt his hand and sent him to bed.

3. Gran went to the dump to drop off a skip full of junk.

4. Fred's box of nuts costs a lot.

9.8 Tracking

Ask your child to find the target words by tracking along each line from left to right with a chopstick or a pencil.

snip pant

s u k p t p a n t v p u n i s n i p g t a

prod still

l p t p r o d f r g ll i d k ll s t i ll a d i

skill floss

s k i t h i ll h i s k i ll r p f l o ss i p m

9.9 Cut and stick

Photocopy this page and cut up the words in each sentence. Working through one sentence at a time, ask your child to read each word and put them in order so they make sense. Then they can stick the words on a piece of paper. Once they've done that, get them to read the sentence again.

1

pet	the	on	is
slug	Jill's	step.	

2

ham	grab	the	grill?
Can	Rex	the	from

3

twin?	Jill	Is	a

9.10 Order and write (letters in words)

Ask your child to order the spellings and write each word, saying each sound as they write it. Then ask them to read the word.

n r g a

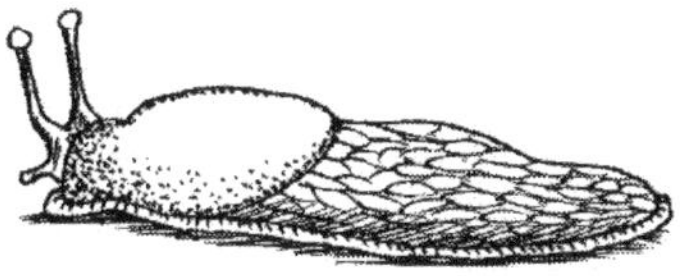

l s u g

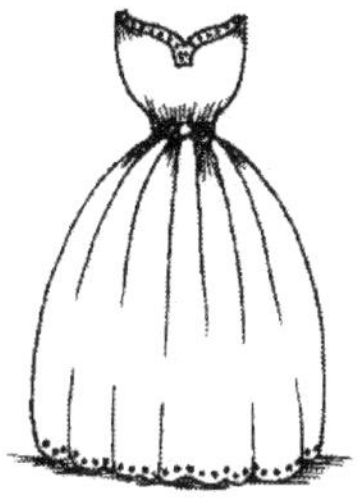

ss e d r

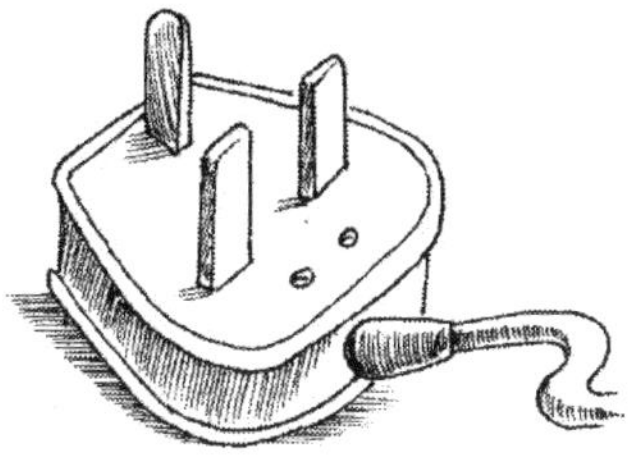

g l p u

+

u l p s

d m r u

9.11 Order and write (words in sentences)

Ask your child to order the words and write the sentences. Tell them to say the sounds as they write each word. When they have written every word in a sentence, ask them to read the sentence.

1. to jump onto the Stan steps. had

2. a trip Bess must to Fred's. plan

3. fat the in pond. The is frog

9.12 Dictation

Tell your child you are going to read a sentence which they will then write on a separate piece of paper or a whiteboard. Firstly, read the whole sentence. Then read each word, one at a time, as your child writes it. Don't forget to remind them to say the sounds of each spelling in each word as they write. When they have written the whole sentence, ask them to read it. Don't do more than one sentence per day.

1. Stig kept his pet slug in a lump of sand.

2. Glen is cross. She has to run to the camp to get some twigs for Mum.

3. The loft is a bit grim. Mum will send Stan to get a box and put the stuff in it.

9.13 Tracing for handwriting practice

Ask your child to practise writing the spellings and saying the sounds as they write each one. Don't forget that < ff > and < ll > are both two-letter spellings for one sound. As your child writes, they should say the sound /f/ or /l/, as the case may be. They should not practise writing the sounds in isolation until after they have been introduced in the word building and word reading exercises.

ll ll ll ll ll ll ll ll ll ll

ff ff ff ff ff ff ff ff ff

b b b b b b b b b

k k k k k k k k k k

9.14 Speed read (CCVC)

How many CCVC (consonant, consonant, vowel, consonant) words can your child read in 20 seconds? Time them and keep a record of how many words they read correctly. You can repeat the activity several times to challenge them to read faster.

swam

flap

club

press

drag

crib

grill

trap

from

smog

glad

snug

Scott

flip

Your record: **Day 1:** **Day 2:** **Day 3:** **Day 4:** **Day 5:**

9.15 Speed read (CCVC)

How many CCVC (consonant, consonant, vowel, consonant) words can your child read in 20 seconds? Time them and keep a record of how many words they read correctly. You can repeat the activity several times to challenge them to read faster.

blab

tram

drum

stuff

drop

slog

dwell

gloss

slit

grim

spill

prod

slum

gran

Your record: **Day 1:** **Day 2:** **Day 3:** **Day 4:** **Day 5:**

9.16 Four in a row game

For the rules of this game, see page 165. Photocopy this page and use it as the board; also photocopy and cut up the counters on page 165.

stub	cliff	dwell	slap	swum	plug	dress	grit
dress	cram	trim	grid	tram	Swiss	drip	Glen
clog	grin	frill	bless	plot	snip	swell	skull
glad	gruff	flag	slug	flan	twig	frog	clap
twin	clam	smell	blob	fluff	slim	grab	brag
flop	Fred	swim	skin	crab	cross	spam	grip
still	fled	sniff	snip	smell	skid	blot	drop

9.17 Memory game

For the rules of the game, see page 165. Photocopy this and the following page and cut up the squares.

trap	troll	Fred	cliff
			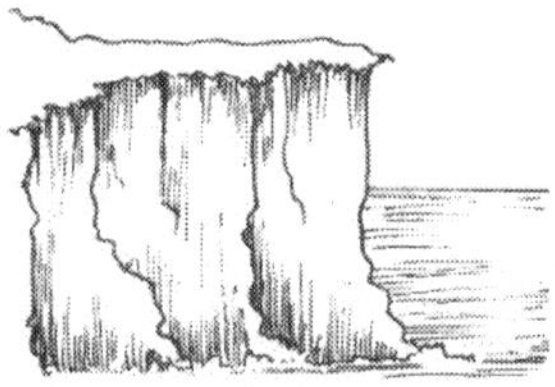
flap	frill	gran	plum

spell	smell	slug	skiff
		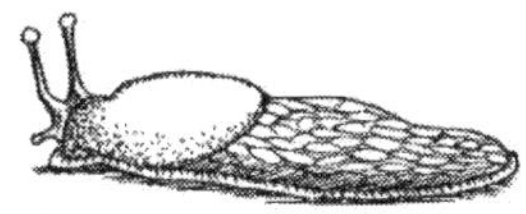	
Jill	stag	stop	tram
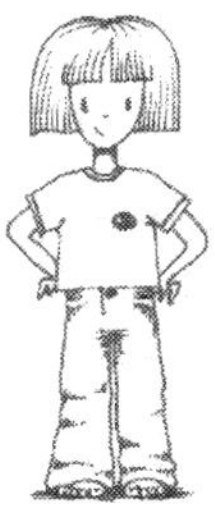			

Unit 10

New sounds-spellings: there are no new sound-spellings in this unit. The unit focuses on segmenting and blending CCVCC, CCCVC, CVCCC and CCCVCC words.

All sounds-spellings: a, i, m, s, t, n, o, p, b, c, g, h, d, e, f, v, k, l, r, u, x, y, j, w, z, ff, ll, ss, zz

Word structure: CCVCC, CCCVC, CVCCC and CCCVCC

High frequency words: is, a, the, I, for, of, are, was, all, to, come, some

10.1 Word building (CCVCC)

Your child is going to build two CCVCC (consonant, consonant, vowel, consonant, consonant) words: 'frost' and 'swift'. For the first word, 'frost', run your chopstick under the lines saying the word very slowly. Don't segment it or separate the sounds. It's your child's job to identify the missing sound. Make sure you are saying the sounds, not the letter names! Emphasise the missing sound by saying it a bit louder (frosT). Now, as your child identifies the sound by saying it, ask them to choose the correct spelling of the missing sound from the 'Sounds/Spellings' box and write it on the line, saying the sound as they write it. Then ask them to write the word, saying the sounds as they do, and read the word. After that, do the same with the word 'swift', stretching out the missing sound (swiiiiift).

Sounds/Spellings
i t

Build the word

f r o s ___

Write the word

___ ___ ___ ___ ___

Build the word

s w ___ f t

Write the word

___ ___ ___ ___ ___

10.2 Word building (CCVCC)

Your child is going to build two CCVCC (consonant, consonant, vowel, consonant, consonant) words: 'slept' and 'slump'. For the first word, 'slept', run your chopstick under the lines saying the word very slowly. Don't segment it or separate the sounds. It's your child's job to identify the missing sound. Make sure you are saying the sounds, not the letter names! Emphasise the missing sound by stretching it out (slllllept). Now, as your child identifies the sound by saying it, ask them to choose the correct spelling of the missing sound from the 'Sounds/Spellings' box and write it on the line, saying the sound as they write it. Then ask them to write the word, saying the sounds as they do, and read the word. After that, do the same with the word 'slump', stretching out the missing sound (slummmmp).

Sounds/Spellings
m l

Build the word

s ___ e p t

Write the word

___ ___ ___ ___ ___

Build the word

s l u ___ p

Write the word

___ ___ ___ ___ ___

10.3 Word building (CCVCC)

Your child is going to build two CCVCC (consonant, consonant, vowel, consonant, consonant) words: 'crabs' and 'spins'. For the first word, 'crabs', run your chopstick under the lines saying the word very slowly. Don't segment it or separate the sounds. It's your child's job to identify the missing sound. Make sure you are saying the sounds, not the letter names! Emphasise the missing sound by stretching it out (crrrrabs). Now, as your child identifies the sound by saying it, ask them to choose the correct spelling of the missing sound from the 'Sounds/Spellings' box and write it on the line, saying the sound as they write it. Then ask them to write the word, saying the sounds as they do, and read the word. After that, do the same with the word 'spins', stretching out the missing sound (spinnnnns).

Sounds/Spellings
r n

Build the word

c ___ a b s

Write the word

___ ___ ___ ___ ___

Build the word

s p i ___ s

Write the word

___ ___ ___ ___ ___

10.4 Word building (CVCCC and CCCVC)

Your child is going to build a CVCCC and a CCCVC word: 'sulks' and 'scrub'. For the first word, 'sulks', run your chopstick under the lines saying the word very slowly. Don't segment it or separate the sounds. It's your child's job to identify the missing sound. Make sure you are saying the sounds, not the letter names! Emphasise the missing sound by stretching it out (sullllks). Now, as your child identifies the sound by saying it, ask them to choose the correct spelling of the missing sound from the 'Sounds/Spellings' box and write it on the line, saying the sound as they write it. Then ask them to write the word, saying the sounds as they do, and read the word. After that, do the same with the word 'scrub', stretching out the missing sound (scrrrrrub).

Sounds/Spellings
r l

Build the word

s u ___ k s

Write the word

___ ___ ___ ___ ___

Build the word

s c ___ u b

Write the word

___ ___ ___ ___ ___

10.5 Word building (CCVCC and CCCVC)

Your child is going to build a CCVCC and a CCCVC word: 'tramp' and 'strap'. For the first word, 'tramp', run your chopstick under the lines saying the word very slowly. Don't segment it or separate the sounds. It's your child's job to identify the missing sound. Make sure you are saying the sounds, not the letter names! Emphasise the missing sound by saying it a bit louder (Tramp). Now, as your child identifies the sound by saying it, ask them to choose the correct spelling of the missing sound from the 'Sounds/Spellings' box and write it on the line, saying the sound as they write it. Then ask them to write the word, saying the sounds as they do, and read the word. After that, do the same with the word 'strap', saying the t a bit louder (sTrap).

Sounds/Spelling
t r

Build the word

t ___ a m p

Write the word

___ ___ ___ ___ ___

Build the word

s ___ r a p

Write the word

___ ___ ___ ___ ___

10.6 Word reading

Ask your child to say the sounds and read the word, and then to match it with the correct picture.

crisp

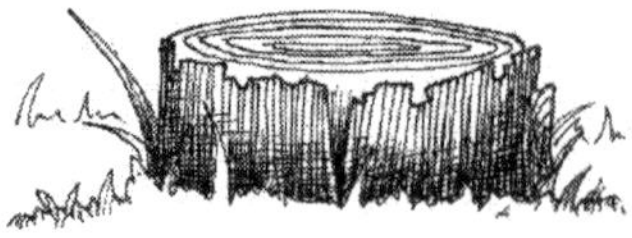

stump

steps

frost

trunk

skunk

10.7 Word reading and writing (CCVCC, CVCCC and CCCVC words)

Ask your child to say the sounds and read each of the words below. When they have read the word successfully, ask them to write it, saying the sounds as they do. When they have written the word, ask them to read it back once more, to make sure the word they wrote was the one they wanted to write.

limps ___ ___ ___ ___ ___

skips ___ ___ ___ ___ ___

stand ___ ___ ___ ___ ___

mumps ___ ___ ___ ___ ___

scrap ___ ___ ___ ___ ___

crept _____ _____ _____ _____ _____

lamps _____ _____ _____ _____ _____

sprig _____ _____ _____ _____ _____

spelt _____ _____ _____ _____ _____

dusts _____ _____ _____ _____ _____

yelps _____ _____ _____ _____ _____

10.8 Sentence reading

Ask your child to read each word in each of the sentences. If they can read the word without sounding out each sound, that's fine. Then ask them to read the sentence again, a bit more quickly this time. Finally, ask them to re-read the sentence once more, this time even more quickly.

1. Grant went to bed and slept until ten.

2. Skunks smell bad. In fact, skunks stink.

3. The twins, Stan and Jeff, swam in the pond and got cramp.

4. Swifts skim the pond to get a drink.

5. Fran left a mess on the steps but Britt swept it all up.

10.9 Tracking

Ask your child to find the target words by tracking along each line from left to right with a chopstick or a pencil.

grins

h s u n g a p z i g r i n s g w n k m l

spelt

z i g l t p s i p s p e l t s u p l g t u

lumps

s l u p z i l u g p s l u n p l u m p s p

10.10 Cut and stick

Photocopy this page and cut up the words in each sentence. Working through one sentence at a time, ask your child to read each word and put them in order so they make sense. Then they can stick the words on a piece of paper. Once they've done that, get them to read the sentence again.

1

up	crept	Sam	the
steps.			

2

not	Vic	well.	has
slept	all	at	

3

hill.	Frank	up	the
sprint	can		

10.11 Order and write (letters in words)

Ask your child to order the spellings and write each word, saying each sound as they write it. Then ask them to read the word.

 l s m u p	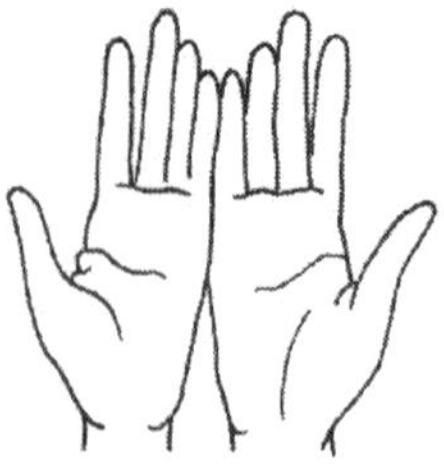 d s a h n	 s s e p t
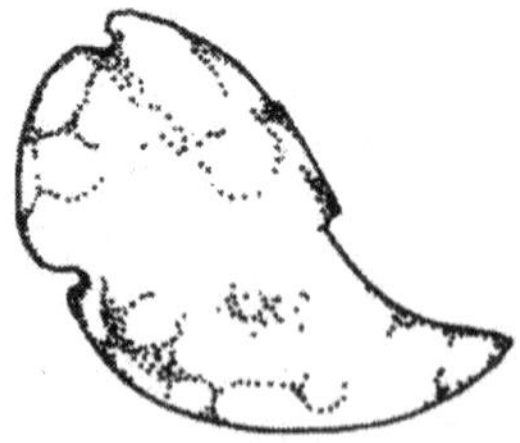 p c r i s	 m t p a s	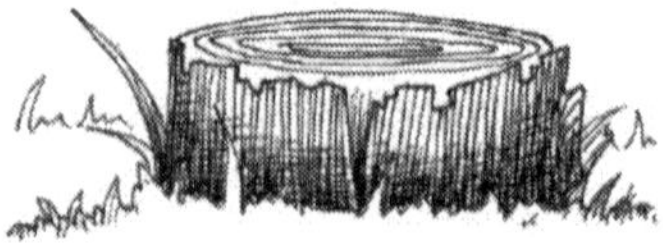 p u t m s

10.12 Dictation

Tell your child you are going to read a sentence which they will then write on a separate piece of paper or a whiteboard. Firstly, read the whole sentence. Then read each word, one at a time, as your child writes it. Don't forget to remind them to say the sounds of each spelling in each word as they write. When they have written the whole sentence, ask them to read it. Don't do more than one sentence per day.

1. Did Jeff send Brett to get some stamps?

2. Pip had some crisps and a can of pop.

3. Jeff's leg is in a splint.

4. Jim grabs the belt and straps himself in.

10.13 Tracing for handwriting practice

Ask your child to practise writing the spellings and saying the sounds as they write each one. As they write, they should say the individual sounds. They should not practise writing the sounds in isolation until they have been introduced in the word building and word reading exercises.

j j j j j j j j j j j j

w w w w w w w w

z z z z z z z z z z

10.14 Speed read

How many words can your child read in 20 seconds? Time them and keep a record of how many words they read correctly. You can repeat the activity several times to challenge them to read faster.

dwelt
stunt
clink
croft
bland
grand
drift
limps
scram
slink
spots
slips
blank
dusts

Your record: **Day 1:** **Day 2:** **Day 3:** **Day 4:** **Day 5:**

10.15 Speed read

How many words can your child read in 20 seconds? Time them and keep a record of how many words they read correctly. You can repeat the activity several times to challenge them to read faster.

trips

frost

sinks

frank

stilts

tramp

stank

stumps

prank

smelt

crisp

sprig

scamp

scram

Your record: **Day 1:** **Day 2:** **Day 3:** **Day 4:** **Day 5:**

10.16 Four in a row game

For the rules of this game, see page 165. Photocopy this page and use it as the board; also photocopy and cut up the counters on page 165.

slept	clamp	bends	costs	mints	lamps	scrub	brisk
claps	cramp	crust	melts	sulks	spent	grunt	dwelt
fists	print	trips	swept	clump	skunk	frisk	swift
spelt	spend	blend	crest	stand	slump	belts	trend
slunk	frond	spots	jumps	clunk	plums	steps	glint
skint	spits	stamp	clips	script	stunt	print	skulk
drink	stomp	winks	crept	spilt	sprat	strum	drops

10.17 Wordsearch

Ask your child to find the following words in the Wordsearch by tracking through each line from left to right. Every time they find a word, ask them to say the sounds and read the word.

blend	clump	cramp	crest	crust	drink
drops	grunt	lamps	plums	print	scrub
skunk	slept	split	stamp	steps	swift

p	a	s	l	e	p	t	i	d	r	o	p	n
b	l	a	m	p	s	i	n	s	c	r	u	b
s	g	s	t	a	m	p	b	r	e	s	k	f
j	l	c	c	r	a	m	p	k	d	r	i	k
s	p	i	t	c	r	u	s	t	r	u	o	w
g	r	u	n	t	a	n	d	p	r	i	n	t
i	s	c	l	u	m	p	s	k	u	n	k	o
b	p	r	i	n	p	o	s	w	i	f	t	i
s	b	l	e	n	d	o	c	r	e	s	t	a
s	l	e	m	p	i	d	v	c	l	e	n	k
s	t	e	p	s	b	l	u	m	s	o	n	f
z	g	g	r	u	n	p	r	i	n	c	m	h
p	l	u	m	s	s	c	r	a	b	t	n	l
a	c	d	r	i	n	k	l	k	r	u	s	t
s	p	l	i	t	j	d	r	o	p	s	k	b

Unit 11

New sound-spellings: Unit 11 introduces several new sound-spelling correspondences

- **the sound /sh/ spelt < sh >**
- **the sound /ch/ spelt <ch>**
- **the sound /th/, voiced and unvoiced, spelt < th >**
- **the sound /k/ spelt < ck >**
- **the sound /w/ spelt < wh >**
- **the sound /ng/ spelt < ng >**
- **the sounds /k/ /w/ spelt < q > < u >**

All sounds-spellings: a, i, m, s, t, n, o, p, b, c, g, h, d, e, f, v, k, l, r, u, x, y, j, w, z, ff, ll, ss, zz

Word structure: CVC, CVCC, CCVC, CCVCC

High frequency words: is, a, the, I, for, of, are, was, all, to, come, some

11.1 Word building: /sh/

Your child is going to build four words: 'wish, 'shop', 'ship' and 'hush'. For the first word, 'wish', run your chopstick under the lines in the 'Build the word' box, saying the word very slowly. Don't segment it or separate the sounds. Make sure you are saying the sounds, not the letter names! Emphasise the sounds by stretching them out. Now ask your child to build the word by writing the missing spelling on the correct line in the box, saying the sound as they write it. Remember that /sh/ is one sound and that the < sh > spelling goes on one line. After that, ask them to say the sounds and read the word. Then ask them to write the word under the 'Write the word' column, saying the sounds as they do, and read the word once again. Keep reminding your child of the target sound-spelling by pointing to the < sh > saying, "This is two letters, but it's one sound. It's /sh/". Then build the other words with your child.

Sounds/Spellings

sh p

Build the word	Write the word
w i ___	___ ___ ___
___ o p	___ ___ ___
sh i ___	___ ___ ___
h u ___	___ ___ ___

11.2 Word building: /sh/

Your child is going to build four words: 'fish, 'shall', 'shed' and 'cash'. For the first word, 'fish', run your chopstick under the lines in the 'Build the word' box, saying the word very slowly. Don't segment it or separate the sounds. Make sure you are saying the sounds, not the letter names! Emphasise the sounds by stretching them out. Now ask your child to build the word by writing the missing spelling on the correct line, saying the sound as they write it. Remember that /sh/ is one sound and that the < sh > spelling goes on one line. After that, ask them to say the sounds and read the word. Then ask them to write the word under the 'Write the word' heading, saying the sounds as they do, and read the word once again. Keep reminding your child of the target sound-spelling by pointing to the < sh > saying, "This is two letters, but it's one sound. It's /sh/". Then build the other words with your child.

Sound/Spelling
sh

Build the word			Write the word
f	i	___	___ ___ ___
___	a	ll	___ ___ ___
___	e	d	___ ___ ___
c	a	___	___ ___ ___

11.3 Word building: /sh/

Your child is going to build four words: 'shift', 'shelf', 'brush' and 'crash'. For the first word, 'shift', run your chopstick under the lines under the 'Build the word' heading, saying the word very slowly. Don't segment it or separate the sounds. Now ask your child to build the word by choosing the correct spellings of the missing sounds from the 'Sounds/Spellings' box and writing them on the lines, saying the sounds separately as they write them. Then ask them to say the sounds and read the word. After that, do the same with the other words.

Sounds/Spellings	Build the word
f sh t i	___ ___ ___ ___
e l f sh	___ ___ ___ ___
r b sh u	___ ___ ___ ___
a c r sh	___ ___ ___ ___

11.4 Word building: /sh/

Your child is going to build four words: 'shred', 'shrub', 'shrug' and 'flush'. For the first word, 'shred', run your chopstick under the lines under the 'Build the word' heading, saying the word very slowly. Don't segment it or separate the sounds. Now ask your child to build the word by choosing the correct spellings of the missing sounds from the Sounds/Spellings box and writing them on the lines, saying the sounds separately as they write them. Then ask them to say the sounds and read the word. After that, do the same with the other words.

Sounds/Spellings	Build the word
d sh r e	___ ___ ___ ___
b u r sh	___ ___ ___ ___
r g sh u	___ ___ ___ ___
l u f sh	___ ___ ___ ___

11.5 Word reading: /sh/

Ask your child to say the sounds and read the word, and then to match it with the correct picture.

shed

rash

wish

shelf

dish

shrub

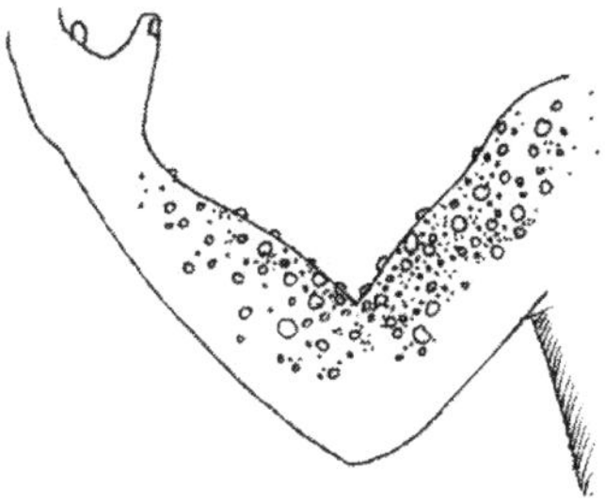

11.6 Word reading and writing: /sh/

Ask your child to say the sounds and read each of the words below. When they have read the word successfully, ask them to write it, saying the sounds as they do. When they have written the word, ask them to read it back once more, to make sure the word they wrote was the one they wanted to write.

shop ___ ___ ___

bash ___ ___ ___

ship ___ ___ ___

rush ___ ___ ___

shell ___ ___ ___

shush ___ ___ ___

shall ___ ___ ___

blush ___ ___ ___ ___

flash ___ ___ ___ ___

splash ___ ___ ___ ___ ___

splosh ___ ___ ___ ___ ___

11.7 Sentence reading: /sh/

Ask your child to read each word in each of the sentences. If they can read the word without sounding out each sound, that's fine. Then ask them to read the sentence again, a bit more quickly this time. Finally, ask them to re-read the sentence once more, this time even more quickly. They might need help with reading the word 'into' – just point to the word and say: "This is 'into', just say 'into' here".

Bash! Crash! Smash! The shop is in a mess.

Mr Bish must shut the shop and get a brush.

The shell fell off the shelf.

Did the bus crash into the shop?

11.8 Tracking: /sh/

Ask your child to find the target word by tracking along each line from left to right with a chopstick or a pencil.

gush

d g o sh g r u sh p s sh i g u sh g m

cash

a c sh b c e g sh c t sh v a t sh c a sh

flash

a i f l o sh s f i l a sh s f l a sh n f m a

11.9 Sentence reading: /sh/

Ask your child to say the sounds and read each word in the sentence, and then answer yes or no by looking at the picture. Remind them that we start a sentence with a capital letter, and that we use a question mark at the end of a question.

Can Mr Shuff shift the van by himself?

Did Stig get a rash from the shrub in the shed?

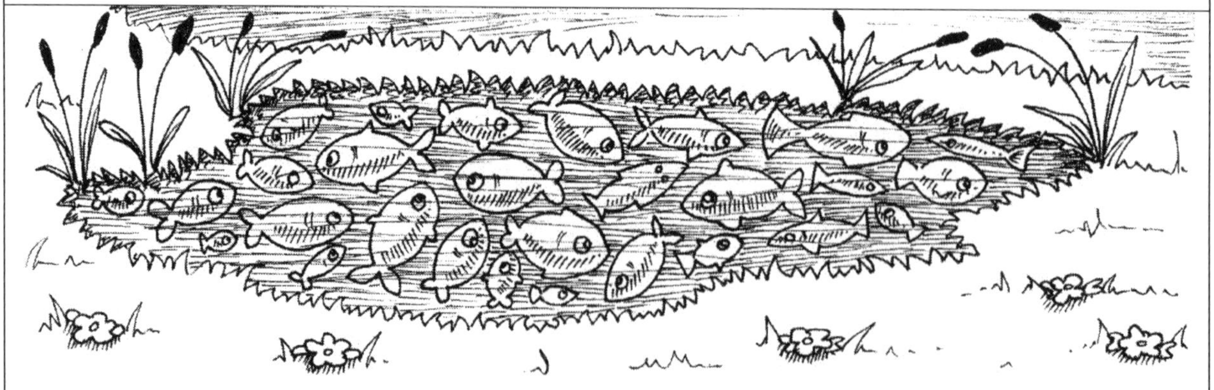

Is the pond full of fish?

11.10 Cut and stick: /sh/

Photocopy this page and cut up the words in each sentence. Working through one sentence at a time, ask your child to read each word and put them in order so they make sense. Then they can stick the words on a piece of paper. Once they've done that, get them to read the sentence again.

1

cat	fresh	The	will
sniff	fish.	the	

2

Dad	shed.	the	will
van	shift	to	the

3

Gran	the	lamp?	Can
mend	the	shelf	on

11.11 Order and write (letters in words): /sh/

Ask your child to order the spellings and write each word, saying each sound as they write it. Then ask them to read the word.

 e ll sh	 e sh d	 p sh o
 sh b r u	 l f sh e	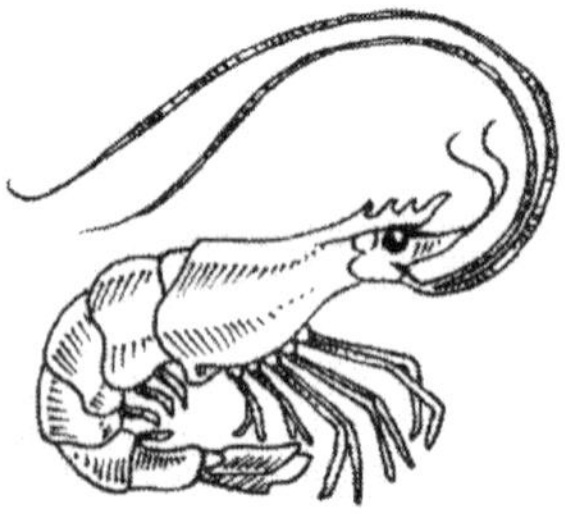 p i sh m r

11.12 Dictation: /sh/

Tell your child you are going to read a sentence which they they will then write on a separate piece of paper or a whiteboard. Firstly, read the whole sentence. Then read each word, one at a time, as your child writes it. Don't forget to remind them to say the sounds of each spelling in each word as they write. When they have written the whole sentence, ask them to read it. Don't do more than one sentence per day.

1 The ship had a clam shell on its flag.

2 The shop sells fresh fish.

3 Can Dad shift the shrub next to the shed?

11.13 Speed read: /sh/

How many words can your child read in 20 seconds? Time them and keep a record of how many words they read correctly. You can repeat the activity several times to challenge them to read faster.

mash cash wish

shell shall

bash

gash

shop

rush

dish

fish

posh shin ash

Your record: Day 1: Day 2: Day 3: Day 4: Day 5:

11.14 Speed read: /sh/

How many words can your child read in 20 seconds? Time them and keep a record of how many words they read correctly. You can repeat the activity several times to challenge them to read faster.

shed
shut
ship
crash
rash
shrug
shred
brush
shrub
Trish
shift
shush
fresh
trash

Your record: **Day 1:** **Day 2:** **Day 3:** **Day 4:** **Day 5:**

11.15 Memory game: /sh/

For the rules of the game, see page 165. Photocopy this and the following page and cut up the squares.

shell	shed	brush	shelf

ship	wish	shrub	fish

dish	crash	shin	shop
		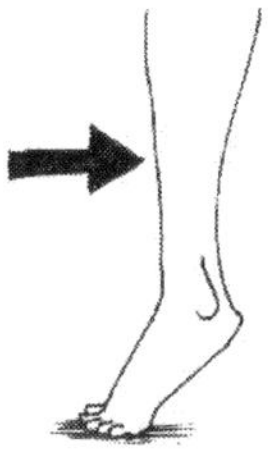	
rash	shush	splash	crush
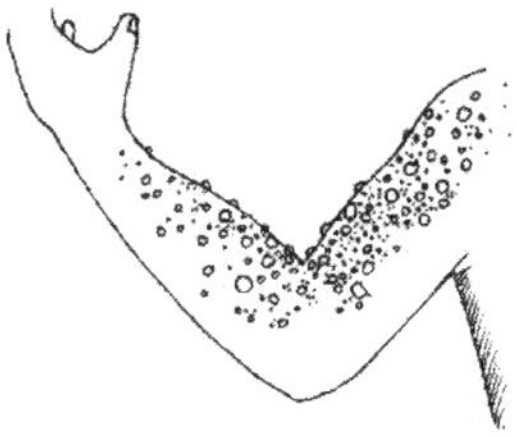			

11.16 Word building: /ch/

Your child is going to build four words: 'such, 'rich', 'chat' and 'chop'. For the first word, 'such', run your chopstick under the lines in the 'Build the word' box, saying the word very slowly. Don't segment it or separate the sounds. Make sure you are saying the sounds, not the letter names! Emphasise the sound /ch/ by saying it a bit louder. Now ask your child to build the word by writing the correct spelling of the missing sound on the line in the 'Build the word' box, saying the sound as they write it. Remember that /ch/ is one sound and that the < ch > spelling goes on one line. After that, ask them to say the sounds and read the word. Then ask them to write the word under the 'Write the word' column, saying the sounds as they do, and read the word once again. Keep reminding your child of the target sound-spelling by pointing to the < ch > saying, "This is two letters, but it's one sound. It's /ch/". Then build the other words with your child.

Sound/Spelling
ch

Build the word	Write the word
s u ___	___ ___ ___
r i ___	___ ___ ___
___ a t	___ ___ ___
___ o p	___ ___ ___

11.17 Word building: /ch/

Your child is going to build four words: 'chill, 'much', 'chum' and 'chip'. For the first word, 'chill', run your chopstick under the lines in the 'Build the word' box, saying the word very slowly. Don't segment it or separate the sounds. Make sure you are saying the sounds, not the letter names! Emphasise the sound /ch/ by saying it a bit louder. Now ask your child to build the word by writing the correct spelling of the missing sound on the line in the 'Build the word' box, saying the sound as they write it. Remember that /ch/ is one sound and that the < ch > spelling goes on one line. After that, ask them to say the sounds and read the word. Then ask them to write the word, saying the sounds as they do, and read the word once again. Keep reminding your child of the target sound-spelling by pointing to the < ch > saying, "This is two letters, but it's one sound. It's /ch/". Then build the other words with your child.

Sound/Spelling
ch

Build the word			Write the word		
___	i	ll	___	___	___
m	u	___	___	___	___
___	u	m	___	___	___
___	i	p	___	___	___

11.18 Word building: /ch/

Your child is going to build four words: 'champ', 'chimp', 'bench' and 'finch'. The only spelling we are now making available for them to see in the 'Sound/Spelling' box is the spelling < ch > for the sound /ch/. This means that you, the parent/carer, need to be particularly careful in stretching out the word. For the first word, 'champ', run your chopstick under the lines in the 'Build the word' box, saying the word very slowly. Don't segment it or separate the sounds. Make sure you are saying the sounds, not the letter names! As your child is already familiar with all the sound-spelling correspondences in each of the words - except, perhaps, /ch/ - you can now ask your child to build the word by writing the correct spelling of each sound on the correct line, saying the sound as they write it. Remember that /ch/ is one sound and that the < ch > spelling goes on one line. After they've built the word, ask them to say the sounds and read the word. Then ask them to write the whole word in the second column, under the 'Write the word' heading, saying the sounds as they do, and read the word once again. Keep reminding your child of the target sound-spelling by pointing to the < ch > saying, "This is two letters, but it's one sound. It's /ch/". Then build the other words with your child.

Sound/Spelling
ch

Build the word	Write the word
___ ___ ___ ___	___ ___ ___ ___
___ ___ ___ ___	___ ___ ___ ___
___ ___ ___ ___	___ ___ ___ ___
___ ___ ___ ___	___ ___ ___ ___

11.19 Word building: /ch/

Your child is going to build four words: 'chest', 'lunch', 'chunk' and 'pinch'. The only spelling we are now making available for them to see is the spelling < ch > for the sound /ch/. This means that you, the parent/carer, need to be particularly careful in stretching out the word. For the first word, 'champ', run your chopstick under the lines in the 'Build the word' box, saying the word very slowly. Don't segment it or separate the sounds. Make sure you are saying the sounds, not the letter names! As your child is already familiar with all the sound-spelling correspondences in each of the words - except, perhaps, /ch/ - you can now ask your child to build the word by writing the correct spelling of each sound on the correct line, saying the sound as they write it. Remember that /ch/ is one sound and that the < ch > spelling goes on one line. After they've built the word, ask them to say the sounds and read the word. Then ask them to write the whole word in the second column, under the 'Write the word' heading, saying the sounds as they do, and read the word once again. Keep reminding your child of the target sound-spelling by pointing to the < ch > saying, "This is two letters, but it's one sound. It's /ch/". Then build the other words with your child.

Sound/Spelling
ch

Build the word	Write the word
___ ___ ___ ___	___ ___ ___ ___
___ ___ ___ ___	___ ___ ___ ___
___ ___ ___ ___	___ ___ ___ ___
___ ___ ___ ___	___ ___ ___ ___

11.20 Word reading: /ch/

Ask your child to say the sounds and read the word, and then to match it with the correct picture.

chest

bench

champ

finch

pinch

lunch

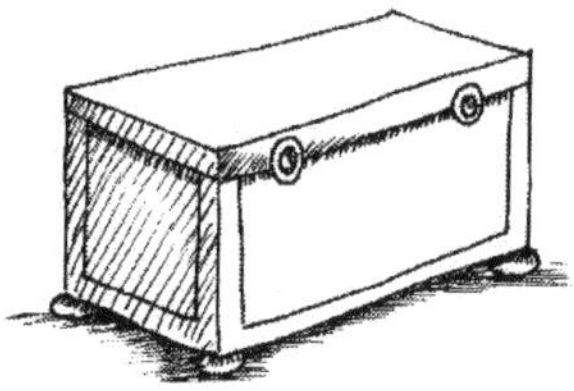

11.21 Word reading and writing: /ch/

Ask your child to say the sounds and read each of the words below. When they have read the word successfully, ask them to write it, saying the sounds as they do. When they have written the word, ask them to read it back once more, to make sure the word they wrote was the one they wanted to write.

chat ___ ___ ___

chill ___ ___ ___

chin ___ ___ ___

much ___ ___ ___

rich ___ ___ ___

bunch ___ ___ ___ ___

chimp ___ ___ ___ ___

munch ___ ___ ___ ___

chunk ___ ___ ___ ___

drench ___ ___ ___ ___ ___

flinch ___ ___ ___ ___ ___

11.22 Sentence reading: /ch/

Ask your child to say the sounds and read each word in the sentence, and then to match it with the correct picture.

The chimp had chips for lunch.

Can Chad chop some logs and set up a bench?

Josh has a bit of a chill on his chest.

11.23 Sentence reading: /ch/

Ask your child to say the sounds and read each word in the sentence, and then answer yes or no by looking at the picture. Remind them that we start a sentence with a capital letter, and that we use a question mark at the end of a question.

Did the finch sit on the bench?

Did the chimp punch himself on the chest?

Did Chas get a clap from his pals in the stand? Is Chas the chess champ?

11.24 Tracking: /ch/

Ask your child to find the target word by tracking along each line from left to right with a chopstick or a pencil.

much

d m o ch g m u sh p s ch i m u ch g m

rich

r c ch b c i r ch c t sh r i ch c i ch u sh

chimp

i m ch l p ch s ch i m p sh m p ch a m

11.25 Tracking: /ch/

Ask your child to find the target word by tracking along each line from left to right with a chopstick or a pencil.

chop

d p o ch p r o ch p s ch i p o ch o p

chill

a i ch ll c e i ch ch t ll v ch i ll c a sh

bunch

ch i b l n ch s b u n ch s b l a ch n f n

11.26 Cut and stick: /ch/

Photocopy this page and cut up the words in each sentence. Working through one sentence at a time, ask your child to read each word and put them in order so they make sense. Then they can stick the words on a piece of paper. Once they've done that, get them to read the sentence again.

1

Chad	rash	a	had
chest.	on	his	

2

had	lunch.	I	wish
for	chips	I	

3

chop	logs	Jeff?	Can
some	for	Chad	

11.27 Order and write (letters in words): /ch/

Ask your child to order the spellings and write each word, saying each sound as they write it. Then ask them to read the word.

o ch p

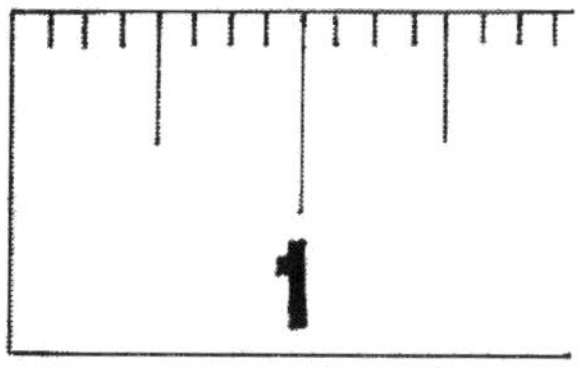

ch n i

s ch p i

l n ch u

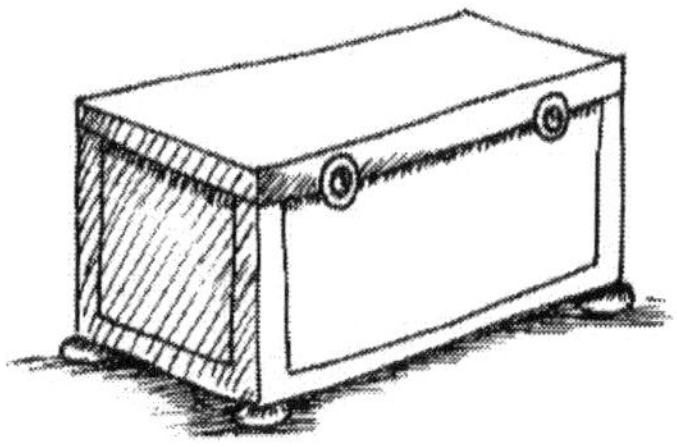

t s ch e

i ch r

11.28 Dictation: /ch/

Tell your child you are going to read some sentences, which they will then write on a separate piece of paper or a whiteboard. Firstly, read the whole sentence. Then read each word, one at a time, as your child writes it. Don't forget to remind them to say the sounds of each spelling in each word as they write. When they have written the whole sentence, ask them to read it. Don't do more than one section per day.

1. Dad had to mop Chad's chin.

2. Chip is Chad's pal. He has such a lot of cash. He is rich.

3. A tench is a fish. It has red spots on its fins.

4. Chas sat on a bench and had fish and chips for lunch.

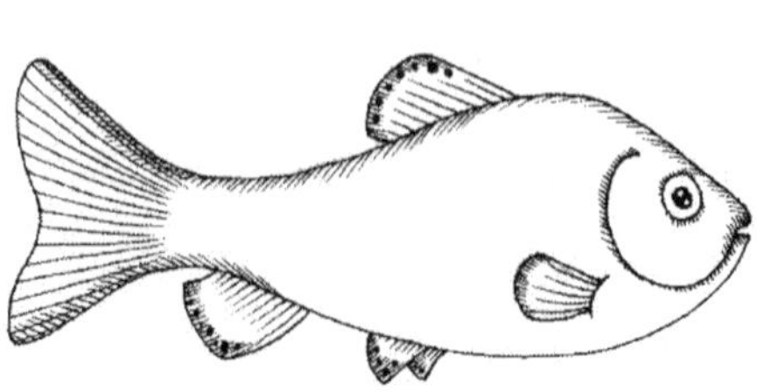

11.29 Speed read: /ch/

How many words can your child read in 20 seconds? Time them and keep a record of how many words they read correctly. You can repeat the activity several times to challenge them to read faster.

chat
chip
such
chill
much
chins
chess
rich
chum
chops
chin
chap
chips
chop

Your record: **Day 1:** **Day 2:** **Day 3:** **Day 4:** **Day 5:**

11.30 Speed read: /ch/

How many words can your child read in 20 seconds? Time them and keep a record of how many words they read correctly. You can repeat the activity several times to challenge them to read faster.

chips

chunk

lunch

tench

bunch

chest

inch

chunks

bench

punch

chimps

champs

munch

finch

Your record: **Day 1:** **Day 2:** **Day 3:** **Day 4:** **Day 5:**

11.31 Memory game: /ch/

For the rules of the game, see page 165. Photocopy this and the following page and cut up the squares.

bench	chop	finch	rich

punch	chimp	chess	chest
			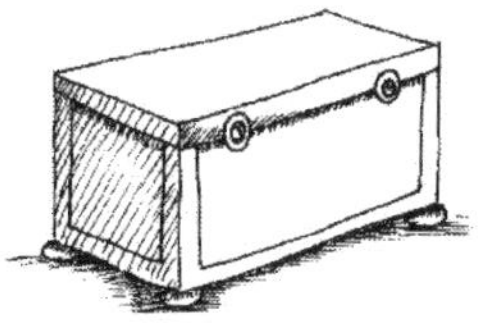

champ	chips	chin	munch
		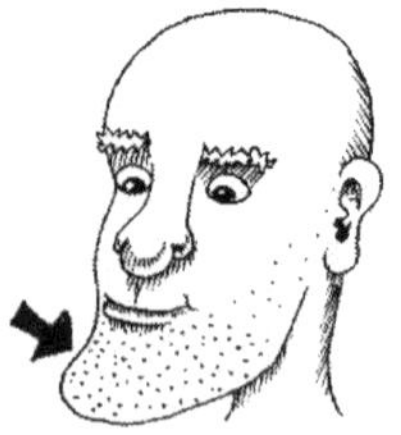	
inch	lunch	pinch	bunch
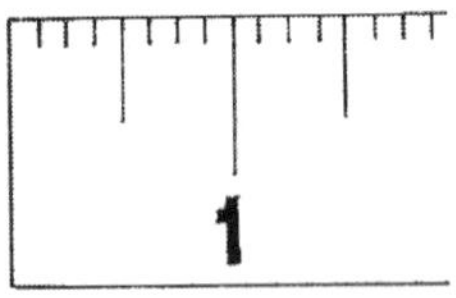			

11.32 Four in a row game: /sh/ and /ch/

This game provides practice in recycling and differentiating the spellings < sh > and < ch >. For the rules of the game, see page 165. Photocopy this page and use it as the board; also photocopy and cut up the counters on page 165.

much	tosh	dash	splosh	chimp	bunch	rash	rich
dish	munch	shrubs	Tash	hash	shreds	chest	shed
splish	shrug	fresh	shells	splash	such	shelf	wish
sheds	shush	chins	crash	ships	shut	shop	hush
mesh	slash	shift	champ	crush	Trish	chunk	trench
bash	shots	dish	mush	chimp	fish	sash	chips
rush	Josh	chats	cash	chum	lash	chops	posh

11.33 Word building: /th/ (unvoiced)

Your child is going to build four words: 'thud', 'moth', 'thin' and 'Kath'. For the first word, 'thud', run your chopstick under the lines in the 'Build the word' box, saying the word very slowly. Don't segment it or separate the sounds. Make sure you are saying the sounds, not the letter names! Emphasise the sound /th/ by stretching it out a bit. Now ask your child to build the word by writing the correct spelling of the sound on the line in the 'Build the word' box, saying the sound as they write it. Remember that /th/ is one sound and that the < th > spelling goes on one line. After that, ask them to write the word under the 'Write the word' heading, saying the sounds as they do, and read the word once again. Keep reminding your child of the target sound-spelling by pointing to the < th > saying, "This is two letters, but it's one sound. It's /th/". Then build the other words with your child.

Sound/Spelling
th

Build the word			Write the word
___	u	d	___ ___ ___
m	o	___	___ ___ ___
___	i	n	___ ___ ___
K	a	___	___ ___ ___

11.34 Word building: /th/ (unvoiced)

Your child is going to build four words: 'tenth', 'fifth', 'broth' and 'throb'. The only spelling we are now making available for your child in the 'Sound/Spelling' box is the spelling < th > for the sound /th/. This means that you, the parent/carer, need to be particularly careful in stretching out the word. For the first word, 'tenth', run chopstick under the lines in the 'Build the word' box, saying the word very slowly. Don't segment it or separate the sounds. Make sure you are saying the sounds, not the letter names! As your child is already familiar with all the sound-spelling correspondences in each of the words except, perhaps, /th/, you can ask them to build the word by writing the correct spelling of each sound on the correct line, saying the sound as they write it. Remember that /th/ is one sound and that the < th > spelling goes on one line. After they've built the word, ask them to say the sounds and read the word. Then ask them to write the whole word in the second column, under the 'Write the word' heading, saying the sounds as they do, and read the word once again. Keep reminding your child of the target sound-spelling by pointing to the < th > saying, "This is two letters, but it's one sound. It's /th/". Then build the other words with your child.

Sound/Spelling
th

Build the word	Write the word
___ ___ ___ ___	___ ___ ___ ___
___ ___ ___ ___	___ ___ ___ ___
___ ___ ___ ___	___ ___ ___ ___
___ ___ ___ ___	___ ___ ___ ___

11.35 Word building: /th/ (unvoiced)

Your child is going to build four words: 'thump', 'cloth', 'depth' and 'froth'. The only spelling we are now making available for your child in the 'Sound/Spelling' box is the spelling < th > for the sound /th/. This means that you, the parent/carer, need to be particularly careful in stretching out the word. For the first word, 'tenth', run chopstick under the lines in the 'Build the word' box, saying the word very slowly. Don't segment it or separate the sounds. Make sure you are saying the sounds, not the letter names! As your child is already familiar with all the sound-spelling correspondences in each of the words except, perhaps, /th/, you can ask them to build the word by writing the correct spelling of each sound on the correct line, saying the sound as they write it. Remember that /th/ is one sound and that the < th > spelling goes on one line. After they've built the word, ask them to say the sounds and read the word. Then ask them to write the whole word in the second column, under the 'Write the word' heading, saying the sounds as they do, and read the word once again. Keep reminding your child of the target sound-spelling by pointing to the < th > saying, "This is two letters, but it's one sound. It's /th/". Then build the other words with your child.

Sound/Spelling

th

Build the word	Write the word
___ ___ ___ ___	___ ___ ___ ___
___ ___ ___ ___	___ ___ ___ ___
___ ___ ___ ___	___ ___ ___ ___
___ ___ ___ ___	___ ___ ___ ___

11.36 Word building: /th/ (voiced)

When the sound /th/ is voiced, this is usually at the beginning of a deictic word - that is to say, a word that is pointing to a particular time, place or situation. Typical examples are 'this', 'that', 'them', 'then', 'these', 'those' and 'there'. This course doesn't deal with the last three words because the sound-spelling correspondences go beyond its remit. So in this activity, your child is going to build the words 'this', 'that', 'them' and 'then'. For the first word, 'this', run your chopstick under the lines in the 'Build the word' box, saying the word very slowly. Don't segment it or separate the sounds. Make sure you are saying the sounds, not the letter names! Emphasise the sound /th/ by stretching it out a bit. Now ask your child to build the word by writing the correct spelling of the sound on the line in the 'Build the word' box, saying the sound as they write it. Remember that /th/ is one sound and that the < th > spelling goes on one line. After that, ask them to write the word under the 'Write the word' heading, saying the sounds as they do, and read the word once again. Keep reminding your child of the target sound-spelling by pointing to the < th > saying, "This is two letters, but it's one sound. It's /th/".
Then build the other words with your child.

Sound/Spelling
th

Build the word			Write the word		
___	i	s	___	___	___
___	a	t	___	___	___
___	e	m	___	___	___
___	e	n	___	___	___

11.37 Word reading and writing: /th/

Ask your child to say the sounds and read each of the words below. When they have read the word successfully, ask them to write it, saying the sounds as they do. When they have written the word, ask them to read it back once more, to make sure the word they wrote was the one they wanted to write. This reading and writing activity includes both the unvoiced and the voiced spelling < th >. Remember that, in each word, < th > is two letters, but it is one sound.

moth ____ ____ ____

cloth ____ ____ ____ ____

thump ____ ____ ____ ____

broth ____ ____ ____ ____

fifth ____ ____ ____ ____

this ___ ___ ___

that ___ ___ ___

then ___ ___ ___

them ___ ___ ___

with ___ ___ ___

11.38 Sentence reading: /th/

Ask your child to say the sounds and read each word in the sentence, and then to match it with the correct picture.

I think that the sun will melt the thick frost.
Thanks to Shep, Beth can swim a width.
Thad is a big fan of moths. He has lots of them.

11.39 Tracking: /th/

Ask your child to find the target words by tracking along each line from left to right with a chopstick or a pencil.

thump

p u th p m o sh u th i m p o th u m p

thrift

th i f t c r i t ch th r i f t th v th i f t a

this that

th i b l n th a t u n th s b th a th n f n
th t a o s th i s th i z ch a sh th

11.40 Sentence reading: /th/

Ask your child to say the sounds and read each word in the sentence, and then answer yes or no by looking at the picture. Remind them that we start a sentence with a capital letter, and that we use a question mark at the end of a question.

Can Thad swim six widths of the pond?

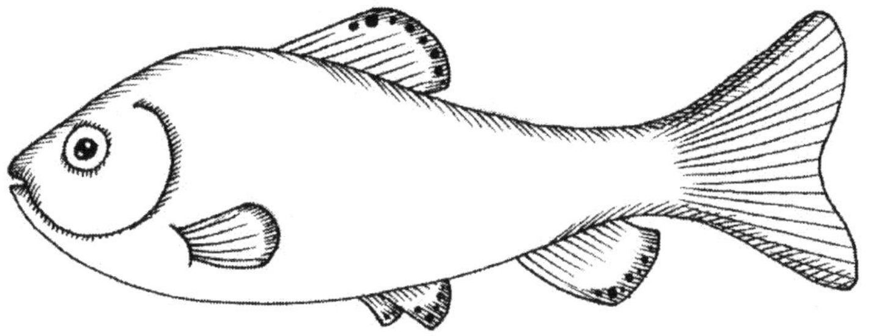

Has a tench got red spots on its fins?

I think that Beth can get the froth off the pond. Can she?

11.41 Dictation: /th/

Tell your child you are going to read a sentence which they will then write on a separate piece of paper or a whiteboard. Firstly, read the whole sentence. Then read each word, one at a time, as your child writes it. Don't forget to remind them to say the sounds of each spelling in each word as they write. When they have written the whole sentence, ask them to read it. Don't do more than one sentence per day.

1. Seth thinks he is a bit thin.

2. Beth went with Ben to the thrift shop.

3. The chimp fell off the shelf with a thud.

11.42 Speed read: /th/

How many words can your child read in 20 seconds? Time them and keep a record of how many words they read correctly. You can repeat the activity several times to challenge them to read faster.

thin
think
throb
moth
broth
depth
sixth
cloth
thank
tenth
width
thud
fifth
froth

Your record: **Day 1:** **Day 2:** **Day 3:** **Day 4:** **Day 5:**

11.43 Wordsearch: /th/

Find the following words in the Wordsearch by tracking through each line from left to right. Remember that sometimes we spell a sound with two letters; in this Wordsearch, you will see some two-letter spellings. When the two letters are in the same square, they represent one sound. Every time the child finds a word in the Wordsearch, ask them to say the sounds and read the word.

broth	cloth	depth	fifth	froth	moth
tenth	that	them	then	thick	thin
think	this	throb	thud	thump	width

t	th	u	d	ss	p	m	o	th	c	l	o	p
b	o	ck	a	th	a	m	i	n	th	i	n	o
h	o	t	e	n	th	f	i	f	th	th	u	p
b	r	o	th	r	o	b	r	th	r	o	b	o
m	o	ck	a	n	th	u	m	p	i	s	o	n
c	l	o	th	t	e	n	d	e	p	th	f	k
b	r	o	z	ll	th	i	s	w	f	i	th	u
ss	i	f	r	o	th	s	r	o	th	o	r	s
th	i	m	s	c	o	th	ss	o	th	i	n	k
ff	i	b	ck	o	th	e	th	a	t	c	o	th
g	u	w	i	d	th	o	m	t	e	n	t	i
ll	e	n	t	i	ck	t	e	n	f	ck	a	th
th	e	n	w	i	d	n	th	i	ck	ff	i	ll
b	e	zz	i	ll	e	n	t	th	e	m	a	p

11.44 Word building: < ck > for /k/

The spelling < ck > is another way of spelling the sound /k/. So far, we've had two different ways of spelling the sound: < c > and < k >. This new spelling adds yet another way of spelling the sound. Say to your child, "This is another way of spelling the sound /k/". As before, your child is going to build four words: 'rock', 'lick', 'neck' and 'thick'. For the first word, 'rock', do exactly as you've done before: say the word in the 'Build the word' box as you run your chopstick under each sound. You can't stretch out the sound /k/, so you'll need to say it with a bit more emphasis. Now ask your child to build the word by writing the spelling of the sound /k/ on the line in the 'Build the word' box, saying the sound as they write it. Remember that /k/ is one sound and that the < ck > spelling goes on one line. After that, ask them to say the sounds and read the word. Then ask them to write the word under the 'Write the word' heading, saying the sounds as they do, and read the word once again. Keep reminding your child of the target sound-spelling by pointing to the < ck > saying, "This is two letters, but it's one sound. It's /k/".

Sound/Spelling
ck

Build the word	Write the word
r o ___	___ ___ ___
l i ___	___ ___ ___
n e ___	___ ___ ___
th i ___	___ ___ ___

11.45 Word building: < ck > for /k/

The spelling < ck > is another way of spelling the sound /k/. So far, we've had two different ways of spelling the sound: < c > and < k >. This new spelling adds yet another way of spelling the sound. Say to your child, "This is another way of spelling the sound /k/". As before, your child is going to build four words: 'check', 'shock', 'chick' and 'kick'. For the first word, 'check', do exactly as you've done before: say the word in the 'Build the word' box as you run your chopstick under each sound. You can't stretch out the sound /k/, so you'll need to say it with a bit more emphasis. Now ask your child to build the word by writing the spelling of the sound /k/ on the line in the 'Build the word' box,, saying the sound as they write it. Remember that /k/ is one sound and that the < ck > spelling goes on one line. After that, ask them to say the sounds and read the word. Then ask them to write the word under the 'Write the word' column, saying the sounds as they do, and read the word once again. Keep reminding your child of the target sound-spelling by pointing to the < ck > saying, "This is two letters, but it's one sound. It's /k/".

Sound/Spelling
ck

Build the word			Write the word		
ch	e	___	___	___	___
sh	o	___	___	___	___
ch	i	___	___	___	___
k	i	___	___	___	___

11.46 Word building: < ck > for /k/

Your child is going to build three words: 'slack', 'clock' and 'truck'. The only spelling we are now making available for your child in the 'Sound/Spelling' box is the spelling < ck > for the sound /k/. This means that you, the parent/carer, need to be particularly careful in stretching out the word. For the first word, 'slack', run chopstick under the lines in the 'Build the word' box, saying the word very slowly. Don't segment it or separate the sounds. Make sure you are saying the sounds, not the letter names! As your child is already familiar with all the sound-spelling correspondences in each of the words except the spelling of /k/, you can ask them to build the word by writing the correct spelling of each sound on the correct line, saying the sound as they write it. Remember that /k/ is one sound and that the < ck > spelling goes on one line. After they've built the word, ask them to say the sounds and read the word. Then ask them to write the whole word in the second column, under the 'Write the word' heading, saying the sounds as they do, and read the word once again. Keep reminding your child of the target sound-spelling by pointing to the < ck > saying, "This is two letters, but it's one sound. It's /k/". Then build the other words with your child.

Sound/Spelling
ck

Build the word	Write the word
___ ___ ___ ___	___ ___ ___ ___
___ ___ ___ ___	___ ___ ___ ___
___ ___ ___ ___	___ ___ ___ ___

11.47 Word reading: < ck > for /k/

Ask your child to say the sounds and read the word, and then to match it with the correct picture.

duck

neck

sock

shack

truck

stick

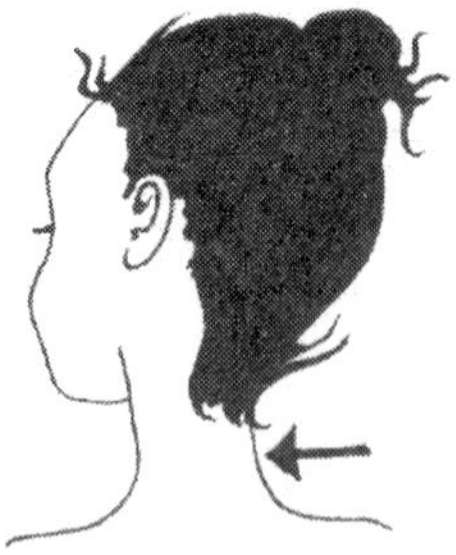

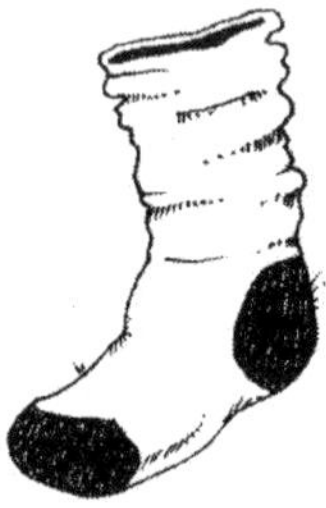

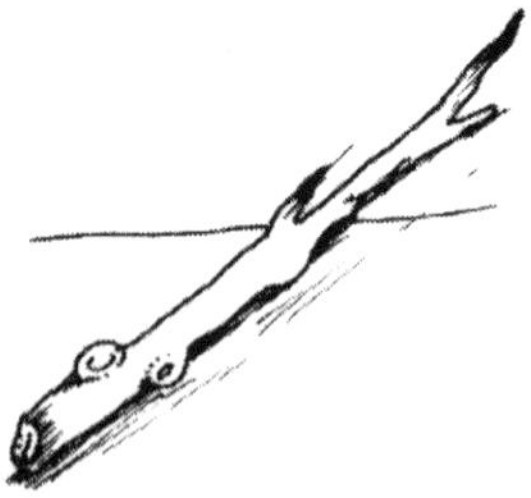

11.48 Word reading and writing: < ck > for /k/

Ask your child to say the sounds and read each of the words below. When they have read the word successfully, ask them to write it, saying the sounds as they do. When they have written the word, ask them to read it back once more, to make sure the word they wrote was the one they wanted to write. You can also use these words as a spelling quiz later. Give your child a piece of paper or a whiteboard. Dictate the word and ask them to write it, saying the sounds as they do. When they've written the word, ask them to check that it is correct by reading it back.

lick

pick

luck

tick

lock

Jack ___ ___ ___

kick ___ ___ ___

check ___ ___ ___

clock ___ ___ ___ ___

trick ___ ___ ___ ___

black ___ ___ ___ ___

11.49 Sentence reading: < ck > for /k/

Ask your child to read each word in each of the sentences. If they can read the word without sounding out each sound, that's fine. Then ask your child to read the sentence again, a bit more quickly this time. Finally, ask your child to re-read the sentence once more, this time even more quickly.

This is a shock! A duck, a chick and a chimp in the back of Beth's truck!

Jack has the socks that Rick left in a sack on the back of the bus. That's a bit of luck!

Dad got a pick, a lock, a stick, and a black and red sack and went to the shed.

11.50 Tracking: < ck > for /k/

Ask your child to find the target word by tracking along each line from left to right with a chopstick or a pencil.

pick

d p o ck g p u sh p i ch i p i ck g ck

frock

r f f c i r ck c t sh f r o ck c f ch a ck

chick

i m ch l p ch s ck i m p ch m p ch i ck

11.51 Tracking: < ck > for /k/

Ask your child to find the target word by tracking along each line from left to right with a chopstick or a pencil.

pluck

d p l ck p r u ck p l s ch i p l u ck o p

shock

o i sh ll ck e i sh o ck t sh i ck ck a sh

crack

ck i c r a ck s c a r ck s c r a ck n f n

11.52 Order and write (letters in words): < ck > for /k/

Ask your child to order the spellings and write each word, saying each sound as they write it. Then ask them to read the word.

 ck d u	 o ck l	 o s ck
 ck r t u	 ck s a	 ch ck i

11.53 Dictation: < ck > for /k/

Tell your child you are going to read a sentence which they will then write on a separate piece of paper or a whiteboard. Firstly, read the whole sentence. Then read each word, one at a time, as your child writes it. Don't forget to remind them to say the sounds of each spelling in each word as they write. When they have written the whole sentence, ask them to read it. Don't do more than one sentence per day.

1. Jack and Rick will check on the chicks and the ducks.

2. Can Bill trust Sam to get him the thick, red socks?

3. If Fran's duck is sick, she must get it to the vet.

11.54 Speed read: < ck > for /k/

How many words can your child read in 20 seconds? Time them and keep a record of how many words they read correctly. You can repeat the activity several times to challenge them to read faster.

chick

trick

click

duck

shack

slack

black

shock

truck

block

brick

rock

stick

flock

Your record: **Day 1:** **Day 2:** **Day 3:** **Day 4:** **Day 5:**

11.55 Four in a row game: < th > and < ck >

For the rules of the game, see page 165. Photocopy this page and use it as the board; also photocopy and cut up the counters on page 165.

deck	stack	flick	speck	thank	pluck	thrill	frock
maths	click	froth	crack	broth	thick	slack	throb
fleck	crash	stick	fifth	trick	width	clock	flock
chick	sock	tenth	back	shack	brick	think	check
sixth	pack	shock	depth	pluck	duck	neck	buck
mock	rock	thump	sack	cloth	sick	luck	tick
lick	thin	kick	thud	lock	pick	moth	Jack

11.56 Memory game: < ck > and < ch >

For the rules of the game, see page 165. Photocopy this and the following page and cut up the squares.

chick	back	rock	pick
	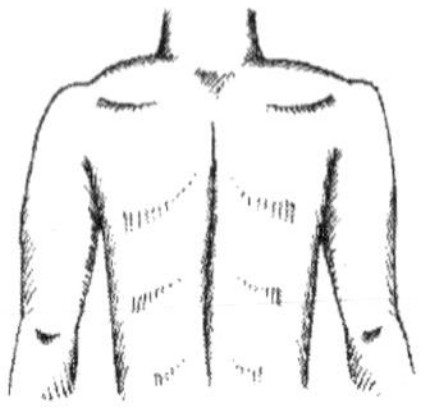		
stick	chess	chest	chimp
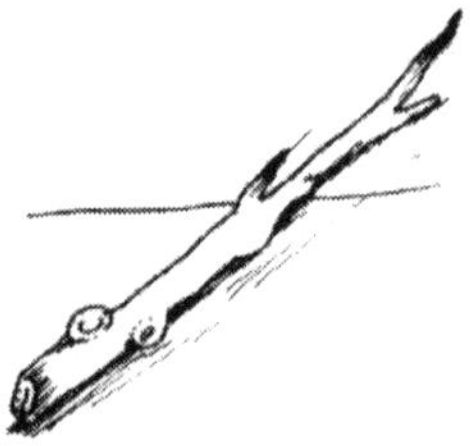		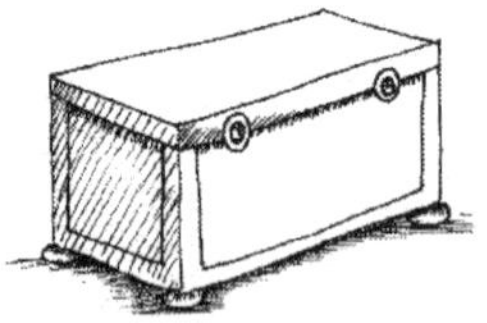	

bench	rich	sack	truck

luck	inch	pack	check
	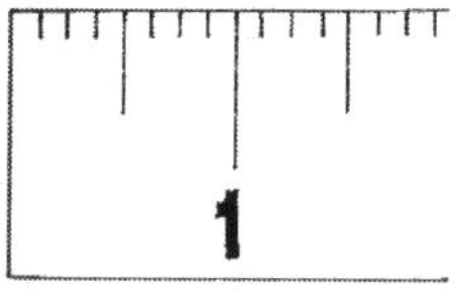		

11.57 Word building: < wh > for /w/

The spelling < wh > is another way of spelling the sound /w/. Say to your child, "This is another way of spelling the sound /w/". Your child is going to build four words: 'when', 'whack', which' and 'whip'. For the first word, 'when', do exactly as you've done before: say the word in the 'Build the word' box as you run your chopstick under each sound. Now ask your child to to use the spelling < wh > for the sound /w/ from the 'Sound/Spelling' box and write it on the line in the 'Build the word' box, saying the sound as they write it. Remember that /w/ is one sound and that the < wh > spelling goes on one line. After that, ask them to say the sounds and read the word. Then ask them to write the word under the 'Write the word' column, saying the sounds as they do, and read the word once again. Keep reminding your child of the target sound-spelling by pointing to the < wh > saying, "This is two letters, but it's one sound. It's /w/".

Sound/Spelling

wh

Build the word	Write the word
___ e n	___ ___ ___
___ a ck	___ ___ ___
___ i ch	___ ___ ___
___ i p	___ ___ ___

11.58 Word reading: < wh > for /w/

Ask your child to say the sounds and read each of the words below. When they have read the word successfully, ask them to write it, saying the sounds as they do. When they have written the word, ask them to read it back once more, to make sure the word they wrote was the one they wanted to write. Remember that /w/ is one sound and that the < wh > spelling goes on one line, as it is two letters, but it is one sound.

whip ___ ___ ___

when ___ ___ ___

which ___ ___ ___

whack ___ ___ ___

whisk ___ ___ ___ ___

11.59 Sentence reading: < wh > for /w/

Ask your child to read each word in each of the sentences. If they can read the word without sounding out each sound, that's fine. Then ask them to read the sentence again, a bit more quickly this time. Finally, ask them to re-read the sentence once more, this time even more quickly. Don't do more than one sentence per day.

If Beth thinks she can whack Josh with a stick, Mum will be cross.

When Jess can sprint up the hill, she will be champ.

When Dad whisks the eggs, Ben will whip the milk into the mix.

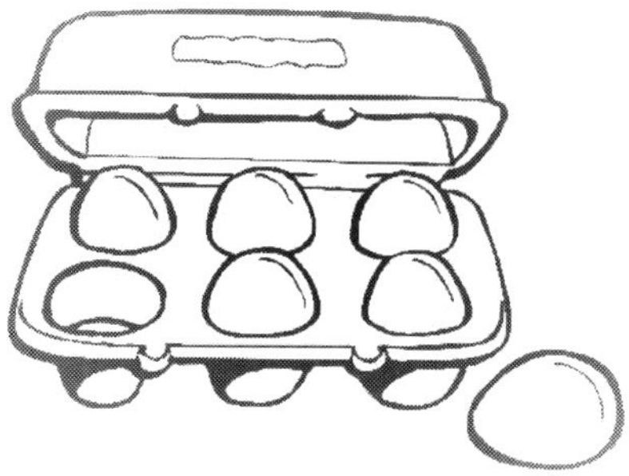

11.60 Tracking: < wh > for /w/

Ask your child to find the target word by tracking along each line from left to right with a chopstick or a pencil.

which

i ch o wh u ch u wh p i wh i ch a m

wham

r c wh a n i wh i m wh r i wh a m wh

whip

i ff wh l ff ch ss wh i m i wh i p wh e t

11.61 Cut and stick: < wh > and < ck >

Photocopy this page and cut up the words in each sentence. Working through one sentence at a time, ask your child to read each word and put them in order so they make sense. Then they can stick the words on a piece of paper. Once they've done that, get them to read the sentence again.

1

back.	Rick	Mum	gets
when	will	up	get

2

Dad	Jack	is	tell
which	will	of	the
ducks	his.		

11.62 Dictation: < wh > for /w/

Tell your child you are going to read a sentence which they will then write on a separate piece of paper or a whiteboard. Firstly, read the whole sentence. Then read each word, one at a time, as your child writes it. Don't forget to remind them to say the sounds of each spelling in each word as they write. When they have written the whole sentence, ask them to read it. Don't do more than one sentence per day.

1. Can Brad whack the ball with his thick bat?

2. It was a shock when the van went into the shed!

3. The man in the ring had a whip in his hand.

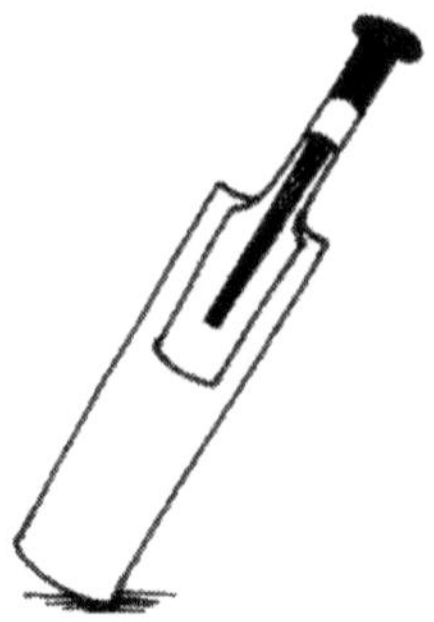

11.63 Wordsearch < wh > and < ck >

Find the following words in the Wordsearch by tracking through each line from left to right. Remember that sometimes we spell a sound with two letters. In this Wordsearch, you will see some two-letter spellings. When the two letters are in the same square, they represent one sound. Every time your child finds a word in the Wordsearch, ask them to say the sounds and read the word.

rock	lick	kick	shock	chick	clock
luck	stick	truck	pluck	check	trick
crack	when	whack	which	whip	whisk

wh	a	ck	l	u	k	t	r	u	ck	ch
r	i	sh	p	p	u	ck	wh	i	s	k
a	r	o	ck	l	u	ck	r	a	ck	a
sh	o	k	ss	t	u	ck	c	r	a	ck
c	l	o	ck	ch	u	wh	e	n	w	i
p	a	n	w	i	p	ff	i	wh	a	c
ch	o	l	i	ck	ch	o	p	sh	e	ck
b	r	i	n	s	t	i	ck	l	o	c
sh	o	ck	p	l	u	ck	z	k	i	ck
s	i	c	ck	r	o	k	w	i	k	s
ll	a	wh	i	p	ch	e	ck	a	wh	e
w	i	n	zz	i	ll	o	n	wh	i	ch
e	t	r	i	ck	d	e	ch	i	ck	p
th	i	s	i	s	th	e	e	n	d	th

11.64 Word building < ng > for /ng/

The sound /ng/ is accent dependent. Many speakers in the UK say it as two separate sounds. In that case, they should not have any problems. as they have already learnt the spellings of the sounds /n/ and /g/. However, for many others throughout the English-speaking world, /ng/ is one sound. If your child says /ng/ as one sound, you can use the following practice exercises. Your child is going to build four words: 'sing', 'thing', 'wing' and 'king'. Build the first word, 'sing', in the normal way: say the word you run your chopstick under each sound in the 'Build the word' box. Emphasise the missing sound by stretching it out. Now ask your child to use the spelling from the 'Sound/Spelling' box and write it on the line in the 'Build the word' box, saying the sound as they write it. Now ask them to say the sound and read the word. Then ask them to write the word under the 'Write the word' column, saying the sounds as they do, and read the word once again. Pointing to the < ng > say, "This is two letters, but it's one sound. It's /ng/". Then build the other words with your child.

Sound/Spelling
ng

Build the word			Write the word
s	i	___	___ ___ ___
th	i	___	___ ___ ___
w	i	___	___ ___ ___
k	i	___	___ ___ ___

11.65 Word building: /ng/

Your child is going to build four words: 'bang', 'long', 'ring' and 'hung'. Build the first word, 'bang', in the normal way by saying the word in the 'Build the word' box as you run your chopstick under each sound. Emphasise the missing sound by stretching it out. Now ask your child to use the spelling from the 'Sound/Spelling' box and write it on the line, saying the sound as they write it. Remember that /ng/ is one sound and that the < ng > spelling goes on one line. After that, ask them to say the sounds and read the word. Then ask them to write the word, saying the sounds as they do, and read the the word once again. Keep reminding your child of the target sound-spelling by pointing to the < ng > saying, "This is two letters, but it's one sound. It's /ng/".

Sound/Spelling
ng

Build the word			Write the word		
b	a	___	___	___	___
l	o	___	___	___	___
r	i	___	___	___	___
h	u	___	___	___	___

11.66 Word building < ng > for /ng/

Your child is going to build three words: 'bring', 'clang' and 'flung'. The only spelling we are now making available for your child in the 'Sound/Spelling' box is the spelling < ng > for the sound /ng/. This means that you, the parent/carer, need to be particularly careful in stretching out the word. For the first word, 'bring', run your chopstick under the lines in the 'Build the word' box, saying the word very slowly. Don't segment it or separate the sounds. Make sure you are saying the sounds, not the letter names! As your child is already familiar with all the sound-spelling correspondences in each of the words except the spelling of /ng/, you can ask now them to build the word by writing the correct spelling of each sound on the correct line in the 'Build the word' box, saying the sound as they write it. Remember that /ng/ is one sound and that the < ng > spelling goes on one line. After they've built the word, ask them to say the sounds and read the word. Then ask them to write the whole word in the second column, under the 'Write the word' heading, saying the sounds as they do, and read the word once again. Keep reminding them of the target sound-spelling by pointing to the < ng > saying, "This is two letters, but it's one sound. It's /ng/". Then build the other words with them.

Sound/Spelling
ng

Build the word	Write the word
___ ___ ___ ___	___ ___ ___ ___
___ ___ ___ ___	___ ___ ___ ___
___ ___ ___ ___	___ ___ ___ ___

11.67 Word reading: < ng > for /ng/

Ask your child to say the sounds and read the word, and then to match it with the correct picture.

bang

king

swing

wing

ring

song

11.68 Word reading and writing: < ng > for /ng/

Ask your child to say the sounds and read each of the words below. When they have read the word successfully, ask them to write it, saying the sounds as they do. When they have written the word, ask them to read it back once more, to make sure the word they wrote was the one they wanted to write.

long ___ ___ ___

sing ___ ___ ___

thing ___ ___ ___

bring ___ ___ ___ ___

sting ___ ___ ___ ___

slang ___ ___ ___ ___

cling ___ ___ ___ ___

lungs ___ ___ ___ ___

11.69 Sentence reading: < ng > for /ng/

Ask your child to read each word in each of the sentences. If they can read the word without sounding out each sound, that's fine. Then ask your child to read the sentence again, a bit more quickly this time. Finally, ask your child to re-read the sentence once more, this time even more quickly. Don't do more than one per day.

Fran's hand is in a sling, but she is still strong.

The twins sat on the swing and sang a song.

Jeff must fling a stick into the pond for his dog Rex.

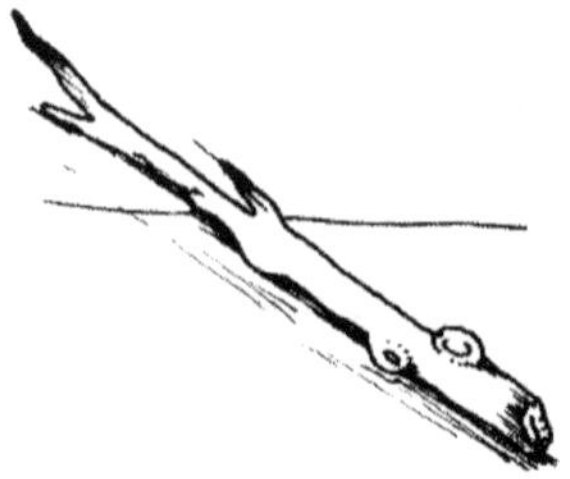

11.70 Tracking: < ng > for /ng/

Ask your child to find the target word by tracking along each line from left to right with a chopstick or a pencil.

ring

u ng o r a ng m u g r i ng i m s i ng m

long

l c ng b l i ng c l sh r o ng l o ng u sh

strong

o m s t o ng s t r i ng p s t r o ng g o

11.71 Dictation: < ng > for /ng/

Tell your child you are going to read a sentence which they will then write on a separate piece of paper or a whiteboard. Firstly, read the whole sentence. Then read each word, one at a time, as your child writes it. Don't forget to remind them to say the sounds of each spelling in each word as they write. When they have written the whole sentence, ask them to read it. Don't do more than one sentence per day.

1. Bring Mum a long bit of string.

2. When Dad gets back, Jill will ring him.

3. Fred kept the swing in the shed till the spring.

11.72 Speed read: < wh > for /wh/ and < ng > for /ng/

How many words can your child read in 20 seconds? Time them and keep a record of how many words they read correctly. You can repeat the activity several times to challenge them to read faster.

bang ring bring

wham whisk

long spring

sting when

whip sling

fling which strong

Your record: **Day 1:** **Day 2:** **Day 3:** **Day 4:** **Day 5:**

11.73 Word building: < q >< u > for /k/ /w/

The spellings < q > and < u > almost always go together in English but they represent the two separate sounds, /k/ and /w/. Your child is going to build four words: 'quit', 'quiz', 'quick' and 'quill'. For the first word, 'quit', run your chopstick under the lines in the 'Build the word' box, saying the word slowly. Don't segment it or separate the sounds. Make sure you are saying the sounds, not the letter names! Remember that if you can't stretch out a sound - such as /k/ or /t/ - you should say it a bit louder. Now ask your child to build the word by writing the correct spelling of the sounds on the lines in the 'Build the word' box, saying each sound as they write it. Remember that < q > represents the sound /k/ and that < u > represents the sound /w/. After that, ask them to say the sounds and read the word. Then ask them to write the whole word under the 'Write the word' column, saying the sounds as they do, and read the word once again.

Sounds/Spellings	
q	u

Build the word	Write the word
___ ___ ___ ___	___ ___ ___ ___
___ ___ ___ ___	___ ___ ___ ___
___ ___ ___ ___	___ ___ ___ ___
___ ___ ___ ___	___ ___ ___ ___

11.74 Word building: < q >< u > for /k/ /w/

The spellings < q > and < u > almost always go together in English but they represent the two separate sounds, /k/ and /w/. Your child is going to build four words: 'quack', 'quest', 'quilt' and 'squid'. For the first word, 'quack', run your chopstick under the lines in the 'Build the word' box, saying the word slowly. Don't segment it or separate the sounds. Make sure you are saying the sounds, not the letter names! Remember that if you can't stretch out a sound - such as /k/ - you should say it a bit louder. Now ask your child to build the word by writing the correct spelling of the sounds on the lines in the box, saying each sound as they write it. Remember that < q > represents the sound /k/ and that < u > represents the sound /w/. After that, ask them to say the sounds and read the word. Then ask them to write the whole word under the 'Write the word' column, saying the sounds as they do, and read the word once again.

Sounds/Spellings

q u

Build the word

Write the word

11.75 Word reading and writing: < q >< u > for /k/ /w/

Ask your child to say the sounds and read each of the words below. When they have read the word successfully, ask them to write it, saying the sounds as they do. When they have written the word, ask them to read it back once more, to make sure the word they wrote was the one they wanted to write. Remember that in 'quack' and 'quick' < ck > are two letters, but they are one sound, so they go on the same line.

quack ____ ____ ____ ____

quick ____ ____ ____ ____

quiz ____ ____ ____ ____

quest ____ ____ ____ ____ ____

quilt ____ ____ ____ ____ ____

squid ____ ____ ____ ____ ____

11.76 Sentence reading: < q >< u > for /k/ /w/

Ask your child to read each word in each of the sentences. If they can read the word without sounding out each sound, that's fine. Then ask your child to read the sentence again, a bit more quickly this time. Finally, ask your child to re-read the sentence once more, this time even more quickly.

A squid sat on a rock and sang a song to a fish.

Quick! Run to the pond. The ducklings are quacking.

It was such a shock when Mum had quins!

11.77 Tracking: < q >< u > for /k/ /w/

Ask your child to find the target word by tracking along each line from left to right with a chopstick or a pencil.

quit

q m o q u i n u q u i t u q i t u t q u i

quilt

q u o q u e n u q u a n d q u i l t u q

quest

q m u q u i ck u q u e s t q u i n u q u

11.78 Cut and stick: < q >< u > for /k/ /w/

Photocopy this page and cut up the words in each sentence. Working through one sentence at a time, ask your child to read each word and put them in order so that they make sense. Then they can stick the words on a piece of paper. Once they've done that, get them to read the sentence again.

1

Run!	flash!	As	a
as	quick		

2

quit	job?	his	Will
Jeff			

3

The	pond.	quacks
in	duck	the

11.79 Dictation: < q >< u > for /k/ /w/

Tell your child you are going to read a sentence which they will then write on a separate piece of paper or a whiteboard. Firstly, read the whole sentence. Then read each word, one at a time, as your child writes it. Don't forget to remind them to say the sounds of each spelling in each word as they write. When they have written the whole sentence, ask them to read it. Don't do more than one per day.

1. Pigs grunt. Robins sing. Ducks quack.

2. When Jack is sick, Mum puts an extra quilt on the bed.

3. Stan cannot quit. He must get to the end of the track and then he can rest.

11.80 Speed read: < th > for /th/ voiced and < q >< u > for /k/ /w/

How many words can your child read in 20 seconds? Time them and keep a record of how many words they read correctly. You can repeat the activity several times to challenge them to read faster.

quill

with

quiz

this

that

quilt

squid

then

quack

quit

them

quest

Your record: **Day 1:** **Day 2:** **Day 3:** **Day 4:** **Day 5:**

Rules for the games

Memory:

Set all the squares face down in rows on a table. In turn, each player chooses two cards and turns them face up. If the word and the picture match, the player wins the pair, **but they have to say the sounds and read the word out loud**! If the two don't match, they are turned face down again and play passes to the next player. The game ends when the last pair has been picked up. The winner is the person with the greatest number of pairs.

Put the set for each unit in a different envelope, and write the unit number on the envelope. If you photocopy the cards for each unit on different coloured paper, it will help you to keep the sets separate.

Four in a row:

This is a game for two players. Each player chooses a set of counters (tops or caps). They take it in turn to read a word on the grid, and place one of their counters on the word they have just read, **but they have to say the sounds and read the word out loud!** The aim of the game is to be the first to form a horizontal, vertical or diagonal line of four of one's own counters.

<u>Counters for four in a row</u>: Stick onto card and cut out.

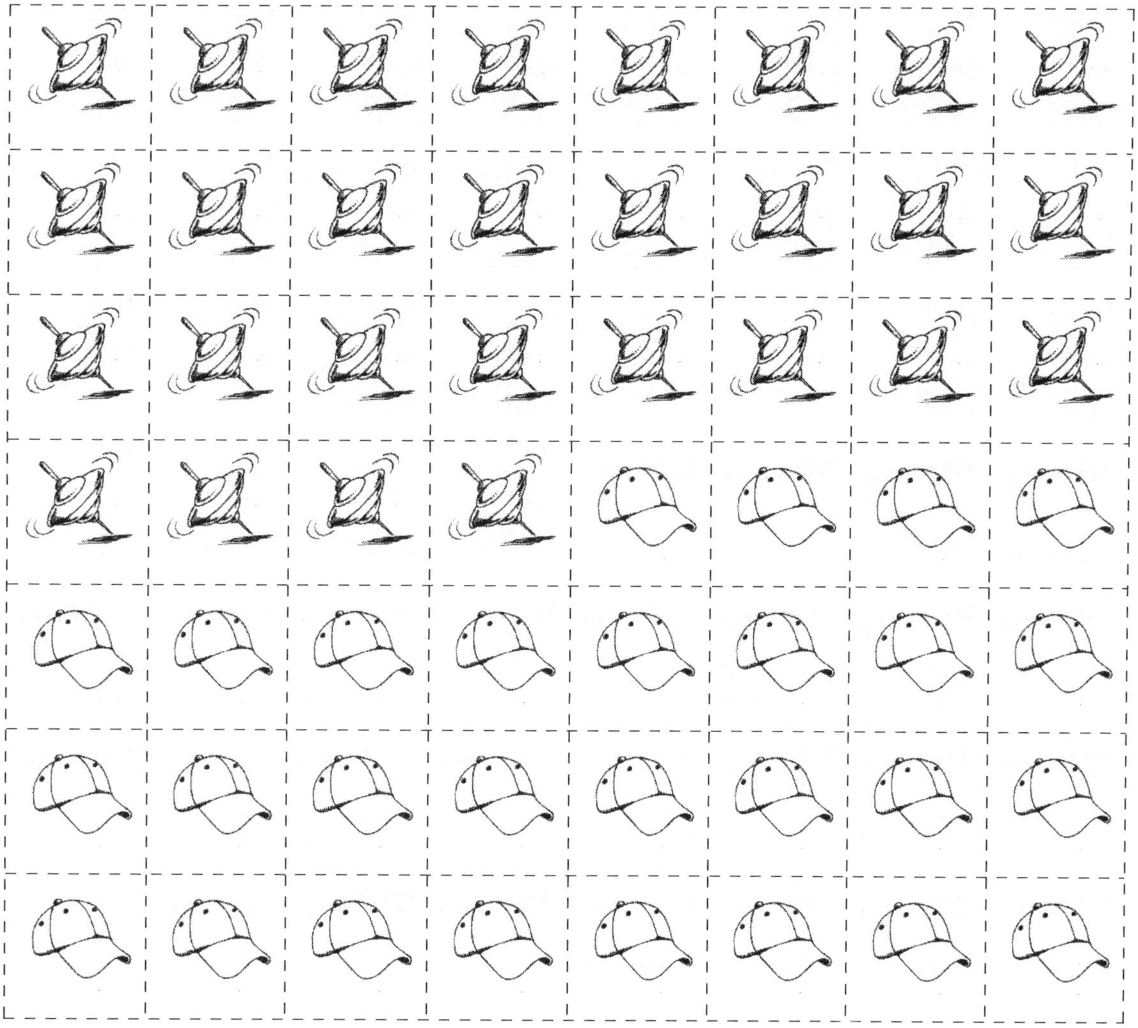

23436518R00095

Printed in Great Britain
by Amazon